Perspectives

Inspiring Essays on Life

Perspectives

Inspiring Essays on Life

by
BAPS Sadhus

SWAMINARAYAN AKSHARPITH
Ahmedabad

Perspectives

Inspiring Essays on Life

Inspirer: HDH Pramukh Swami Maharaj

First Edition: December 2003
First Reprint: June 2004
Second Reprint: May 2007

Copies: 7,000 (Total: 15,000)
Cost: Rs. 60.00
ISBN: 81-7526-236-2

Published & Printed by
Swaminarayan Aksharpith
Shahibaug, Ahmedabad-4, India.

Website: www.swaminarayan.org
kids.baps.org
www.akshardham.com
www.mandir.org

CONTENTS

FAMILY

FRIENDSHIP

SELF HELP

SELF IMPROVEMENT

CULTURE

VEGETARIANISM

ENVIRONMENT

WORLD PEACE

PREFACE

Life is a challenge! Sustaining relationships, developing careers, maintaining health and experiencing internal tranquility have become increasingly difficult. Deadlines, commitments and obligations have burgeoned whereas the day has remained only twenty-four hours long! The dissemination of information by the media has brought forth knowledge of the whole universe to our doorsteps. The internet has made information available at the click of a button and communication occurs 'at the speed of light'.

In olden times, things weren't so pressing. There were only two times on the minds of people. One was 'morning' when the sun rose and the second 'evening' when it set! Today, time has been divided and dissected not only into seconds but micro, nano and picoseconds! Machines scream out incessantly for more and more commands, responding so quickly they compel the user to respond equally rapidly. Contemporary man is unable to keep social, physical or psychological pace with the very machines he has created. Consequently, he has become the tool of his own tools. His existence has become as mechanical and mindless as the instruments he operates.

Today, the young and old, male and female alike, crave guidance, wisdom and insight. They thirst to know answers to questions like "Why do bad things happen to good people?" "Can I change my fate?" "My parents and I suffer a generation gap - what are the solutions?" "How can I improve my self-esteem and confidence?" "How can I improve my memory and concentration?" "How can I manage exam stress?" "Why am I so fearful of crowds or new company?" "How can I take charge of my life?" "How can I become more popular and make more friends?" "I know I have a soul, but what is the proof?" "How can I achieve my childhood dreams?" "When will I experience peace?"

Perspectives is a compilation of 67 short articles on a broad range of subjects pertaining to both the smaller but niggling problems of life to the larger, more profound questions of our existence. The articles are unique in that they are crisp and discuss core issues at the personal, practical level. Each is supported by logic, science, history and inspiring stories and anecdotes. They provide a new perspective to life. The articles also give solid, effective and easy-to-remember guidance. More than forty illustrations lucidly depict the very essence of the articles. They perform the role of a complete food and can be intuited and implemented by any genuinely aspiring human being. The examples given are of real people from all nations, eras and faiths.

- Swaminarayan Aksharpith

PHILANTHROPY...

INTERVIEW: HDH PRAMUKH SWAMI MAHARAJ

Questions submitted to
HDH Pramukh Swamiji Maharaj
by S. Balakrishnan, City Editor,
The Times of India, Mumbai
– April 30, 2001.

Q. Bhagwan Swaminarayan was born near Ayodhya. How come His followers are more in Gujarat than in Uttar Pradesh itself?

A. Bhagwan Swaminarayan left His home at the young age of 11 and began a sojourn of India on foot, through all the *maths*, ashrams and pilgrim places – all the time asking questions and observing closely. Nowhere did he find satisfaction until he met a humble celibate saint called Ramanand Swami in Gujarat. This is where Bhagwan Swaminarayan finally settled and subsequently where the faith has blossomed.

Q. Why is the Swaminarayan movement also called the Akshar Purushottam faith?

A. Just as in the Vaishnav faith we have Radha and Krishna,

Ramchandra and Sita, and in the Shaiv faith we have Shiv and Parvati, similarly in the Swaminarayan faith we have Swami and Narayan wherein Swami is Akshar – the manifest form of God's indestructible, divine abode, Akshardham – and wherein Narayan is Purushottam Himself. However, the name Swaminarayan is frequently used to refer to Bhagwan Swaminarayan alone as Purushottam Himself.

Q. What are the three main characteristics of the Akshar Purushottam philosophy?

A. **1.** Bhagwan Swaminarayan is the supreme personality of Godhead. **2.** Gunatitanand Swami was the manifest form of Akshar and was Bhagwan Swaminarayan's most beloved devotee. **3.** Bhagwan Swaminarayan remains eternally manifest on this earth through a continuous succession of genuine spiritual masters.

Q. The Swaminarayan movement follows the Vaishnavite tradition. Does this mean that it completely rejects the Shaivite tradition of Hinduism?

A. Not at all. We have installed murtis of Shivji in our mandirs.

Q. Both the Vaishnavite and Shaivite traditions derive their inspiration from the Vedas. Then where is the need for two separate streams of Hinduism?

A. Every soul comes with its own karmas. Not every child can be placed in the same class. Students have different aptitudes and preferences – arts, commerce, science. Similarly, individual souls will be comfortable and could progress only in an environment conducive to their personality type. The various religions provide the various environments required.

Q. Even today orthodox Vaishnavites do not offer worship to Shri Ganesh and other deities with the reason that they represent the Shaivite tradition. Is this correct?

A. Along with Shivji, we have also installed *murtis* of Ganeshji and Hanumanji as well in all our mandirs. These are all great deities and are worthy of everyone's respect and reverence.

Q. The Swaminarayan Sampraday has often been criticized for allegedly not giving equal status to men and women. The sadhus of your Sampraday do not even look at women. Aren't women also creations of God? In Hinduism woman is worshipped as Durga, Kali, etc.

A. Women are certainly equal to men. And in many ways their devotion and dedication to God supersedes that of the men! But this does not change how sadhus should conduct themselves in their relation with females. If even householders should not be looking at females other than their own wives – then what to say of sadhus? This is not hatred towards women. We have equal affection and care for all. We cast our eyes down because we respect women. Remember, Lakshman had great affection for Sita, yet, he had never cast his gaze upon her in 14 years of exile and could not recognize her ornaments when they were shown to him by Shri Ramchandra. When a sadhu's goal is so high and after renouncing so much – family, career, wealth and status – he has to be careful to avoid all chances of slipping in the even more precarious area of celibacy. A person who claims he is strong-minded and can drink and drive is nothing but a fool. Similarly, a sadhu who says he will mix freely with the opposite sex and achieve the Almighty is foolish. Yes, people like King Janak reached the Almighty, but examples like his are but a few. And householders like

Janak cannot make effective teachers. How many people of Janak's time looked upon him as a guru or as enlightened? Almost none. Even great, enlightened Masters must teach the masses through their personal example. This Vedic principle is described by Shri Krishna in the Bhagvad Gita [Ch. 3/20-21] and the Shrimad Bhagwatam [11.17.33].

Q. Under your leadership the BAPS has grown by leaps and bounds. What according to you are the three main achievements of your tenure?

A. Through the grace of Bhagwan Swaminarayan and the blessings of my Guru Yogiji Maharaj, inspiring mandirs like the Swaminarayan Mandir in London and the Akshardham Cultural Complex at Gandhinagar, Amdavad, have been built which have revived deep spiritual faith in the people and erected living, *chaitanya* mandirs in their hearts. Many members of the intelligentsia have been drawn to the eternal principles of the Swaminarayan Sampraday and young, dynamic, educated youths have been drawn into the faith's monastic order to serve God and society with total dedication.

Q. Your movement has spent much money and resources in mandir construction. Some people feel that this money would have been better spent in building hospitals and schools for the poor. Please comment.

A. BAPS already spends much on hospitals, schools, youth hostels, medical camps, environment and disaster relief work as we are presently doing in Orissa after the cyclone there in 1999 and in Gujarat where we have adopted 10 villages and earmarked 125 schools for reconstruction after the recent earthquake. But a bird cannot fly with a single wing. It must possess both wings. Similarly, social work needs to be strengthened and fortified with a spiritual foundation or else the entire infrastructure will collapse or get destroyed due to corruption, ego battles, anger, greed and jealousy. Mandirs bring about God consciousness, dedication and devotion. This has given us a dedicated task force of 30,000 volunteers who work with zero administration cost and every rupee donated to us reaches the needy! Mandirs are also hospitals and universities for the treatment and education of one's soul. Millions of people find peace in mandirs – which they do not find in the cinemas, restaurants and discotheques – or even in their own homes! Today, 80% of physical afflictions are psychosomatic. Mandirs redeem people from these mental afflictions and addictions to alcohol and tobacco, etc. so that millions of people are saved from going to hospital at all! We must learn to go to the root of society's problems.

Q. What are your plans for the next ten years?

A. We don't have any plans – we just let things unfold according to God's wish. However, we continually make efforts to spread and nurture faith in God, strengthen moral values and to transform the lives of the people. We will also be building another eco-friendly Akshardham Cultural Complex in New Delhi.

His Holiness Pramukh Swami Maharaj is the head of Bochasanwasi Shri Akshar Purushottam Swaminarayan Sanstha or 'BAPS'.

HAPPINESS...

DEFEAT YOUR DEPRESSION!

The word "stress" used to be a purely engineering term. It dealt with how much pressure and tensile force a piece of metal could bear without deforming. Today, it is also employed as a medical term, referring to the effects on the human body of things such as work pressure, weather, heat, noise, traffic, pollution, financial problems, job interviews, presentations, disagreements, demands for one's time and attention, loss of loved ones, combined with psychological forces such as defeatist, negative and irrational thinking.

Result: deep-seated anxiety, tension and depression on the psychological front and frequent colds, flu, viral and bacterial infections, raised blood pressure, increased heart rate and the onset of cardiovascular disease on the physiological front. The problem is so acute, research shows, that two-thirds of all working days lost are due directly or indirectly to the effects of stress.

Work pressure today and demands to achieve ever and ever tougher goals has burgeoned to the level that the average office goer works three times as hard for only twice the pay compared to twenty years ago! Just look at your own kids! The weight and number of books they lug with them to school today is more than five times what kids carried a decade ago. Shockingly, but predictably, psychiatrists have lately begun to notice symptoms of study-related stress in these minors too! Even more sadly, it has been found that babies within the womb of pregnant and depressed mothers are born with the clinical symptoms of depression, too.

Today is the Age, not of the Space Shuttle, but of Stress!

But this stress epidemic we see spreading throughout the world is not bacterial, viral or physical at root. It is societal and psychical. Most of the infections, raised blood pressures and arterial blockages are symptomatic. This cannot be 'over-stressed'. Stress has developed out of an irrational and blind rush for material success and pleasure with the result of millions of people ending up not with true gold but Fool's Gold – iron pyrite – as did millions of people in South Africa in the 1950s. Materialistic pleasure and success is fool's gold. But ignorance drives ignorance. Numbers drive numbers. "The masses can't be wrong," people reason to themselves. "Let's follow them." Like a flock of sheep which observes one after another of its members step off a cliff with the reasoning that the previous lot couldn't all be wrong. Intelligent human beings are gripped so tightly by the notion that all the rich and famous actors, dancers, singers, models, businessmen, doctors, pilots and IT barons before them can't all be wrong, that they choose to leap off the cliff too! "Insanity in individuals is something rare," said Friedrich Nietzsche, "but in groups, parties, nations, and epochs it is the rule." And did you know that even psychiatrists can suffer from this insanity-related stress and depression?

What will lift this menace that hovers above the heads of almost one and all? It will consist, say experts, of asking ourselves the fundamental question, "Wherein lies our basic self-esteem?" This is a question that hits the root reason behind nearly everything we do. Most people today attempt to build their self-esteem or their self-value on the possession of wealth, fame, status, good looks and talent. But this is foolhardy. "Marilyn Monroe, Mark Rothko, Freddie Prinz, and a multitude of famous suicide victims attest to this grim truth," says Dr. David D. Burns in his best-selling book *Feeling Good.*

All the above people had almost unlimited wealth, fame and status, etc. They were also adored by millions. Yet they threw away their own lives! The fact is, until you love yourself, approve of yourself, endorse and affirm yourself, no amount of wealth or talent or adoration from the masses is going to lift your depression. Learning to love yourself, for what you are – whether you have any achievements or talents behind your name or not is the fundamental basis of peace and true, self-sourced self-esteem. Self-esteem is about accepting and loving yourself together with the world, with all its ups and downs, unconditionally. Understanding this truth, loving it and living by it is the Royal Road to uprooting depression and averting all its physical consequences.

THE COSMIC JOKE

"I'm not very happy most of the time," quipped the hilarious Woody Allen. "The rest of the time I'm not happy at all."

The funny thing about life is that there usually isn't much to laugh about! On the television, the joke is on someone else, so we laugh. Someone's slip-up, someone's struggles, someone's loss of face, someone's sleepless nights. In real life, however, the joke is usually on us. Maybe comedies bring us relief from our own frustrations and failures by drawing our attention to the fictional disasters of others? Or is it that we get to view a reflection of ourselves in those poor souls on the screen before us and a disguised opportunity to see the humorous angle of what happens to all of us; a form of catharsis; a chance to unwind and ease the tension of our tightly twisted, contorted minds?

Laughter, however is not unique to human beings. Monkeys do it all the time! But scientific research using sensitive microphones revealed even mice laugh when turned upside down and tickled on their bellies! And though many scientists refute it, a great number of non-scientists swear that they have seen their pets – be it dog, cat or cow – cry when the animals sensed that something sad had happened in the household. Animals who laugh can certainly cry too. With or without the tears, animals certainly experience despondency like we humans do. Some years back in the US, two lifetime lovers and companions, Charlie and Josephine, were together when Charlie was shot dead in full sight of Josephine by the police after Charlie had become uncontrollable. Josephine collapsed on her knees and lay her head on Charlie's lifeless body. She never arose again. She had not been shot or wounded in any way. Her injuries were

THE COSMIC JOKE

"I'm not very happy most of the time," quipped the hilarious Woody Allen, "because most of the time I'm not happy at all."

The [illegible] thing [illegible] is that there really isn't much to laugh [illegible] the [illegible] the joke is on someone else, so we laugh at [illegible] someone's struggles, someone's loss of face, someone's sleepless [illegible]. In real life, however, the joke is usually on us. Maybe comedies bring us relief from our own frustrations and failures by drawing our attention to the fictional disasters of others? Or is it that we get to view a reflection of ourselves in those poor souls on the [illegible] before us and a disguised opportunity to see the humorous angle of what happens to all of us, a form [illegible] to unwind and ease the tension of our [illegible]

Laughter, however, is not [illegible] Monkeys do it all the [illegible] micro-phones revealed [illegible] and tickled [illegible] a great number of [illegible] pets – be it dog, cat [illegible] that something sad had happened in the [illegible] who laugh can certainly cry. [illegible] animals certainly experience despondency [illegible] years back in the US [illegible] lifetime [illegible] Charlie and Josephine, were together when Charlie was shot dead in full sight of Josephine by the police after Charlie had become uncontrollable. Josephine collapsed on her knees and lay her head on Charlie's lifeless body. She never arose again. She had not been shot or wounded in any way. Her injuries were psychological. The loss of Charlie was too much for her. Her heart stopped beating and her lungs stop breathing. The amazing thing was, Charlie and Josephine were not human beings but a pair of llamas who had escaped from a zoo during a storm!

Man is not much different from his fellow animals. Only his methods differ due to his sophistication and sophistry. Comparison of the human genome with mice and monkeys in particular, have shown that our DNA is shockingly similar to theirs! In fact, we share 98-99% of our DNA with them! It is a humbling discovery. We have shed the fur and the tail, it seems, but not much else. The joke is certainly on us!

Observe the world around you. Most people are crying. Nearly all are lamenting. And over what? Too much money or too little of it! Too much fame or too little of it! Too much isolation or too little of it! Billionaires are beggars in their hearts. Popular people are paupers in their minds.

What a scenario! People have a roof over their heads, clothes to put on their bodies and food enough to fill their stomachs. Yet they want more. Like the peasant farmer in Leo Tolstoy's famous story *How Much Land Does A Man Need?* people continue to run and run in an attempt to gather as much land as they can before the sun sets. Tolstoy's farmer collapsed and died of over-exertion upon returning to collect his accumulated land. He neither acquired the extra land he lusted for, nor did he enjoy the land he already possessed.

Said the great Indian devotional poet Sant Kabir, "I feel amused when I see fish thirsting in the sea." All the avatars and great saints of yore are laughing at the spectacle. It is for them the talk of the town, the shriek of the week – a roaring joke! Theirs is a laughter of cosmic proportions; of magnitude so large that our whining and weeping can find no place before it.

The person who hears this cosmic laughter suddenly awakens. He stops crying, wipes his tears and looks around curiously to see what's so funny. When he realizes the truth he breaks into a fit of uncontrollable mirth as well!

So stop weeping and listen to that cosmic laughter. See the funny point. And laugh your heart out.

THE SECRET ART OF HAPPINESS

It's a rich man's world: Rolls-Royce cars, custom built yachts, five star hotels, mansions, private jets, exquisite jewellery, glamour, style, panache. Oh, how these wealthy barons and beneficiaries must roll in bliss and ecstasy! What heights of fulfilment and satisfaction they must have attained!

Yes and no. Ecstasy – born from a sense of vanity – for a few seconds, maybe. Fulfillment and satisfaction, never.

And do those moments of megalomania, self-worship, swank and grandiosity really consist of happiness or anything even close to it? Or is it a hoax – a deception – like the gold millions of infatuated people collected in South Africa, in the 1900s? The gold they amassed turned out to be iron pyrite – fool's gold.

Do we really so arrogantly believe that all those who are financially poorer than us are also psychologically poorer than us? Remember, poverty is not so much an economic condition as a mental one. Riches are more to do with appreciating fully what one already possesses and that which is irreplaceable: if your house catches fire, save the family photographs first because all the money in the world will not get them back later. Real opulence can never be an empty cradle, even if it is carved of gold. True riches consist of a cradle bouncing with the movements of a baby set to change the world, even though the cradle be a simple, wooden one. And have you ever witnessed the delightful smile of a young baby, though it may be clothed in rags – being the child of poor parents? Haven't you noticed it kick its feet and burst into a wide-open smile upon seeing its mother? And have you ever seen the pleasure and fulfilment on the mother's face upon playing with that beautiful baby?

Love. This is both the hallway and the hallmark of happiness. Not clothes, not cars, not 5-star hotels nor anything else money can buy. Just love. Nothing more, nothing less! Love says it all, does it all, fills it all – the heart, mind and soul!

Happiness is not reserved for the rich and famous. Happiness is one thing God has reserved for all. The number of friends and acquaintances you have is of little account. The quality of friends – even just one – a person one can be oneself with, a person one can really trust with one's secrets, is more than enough.

In the final analysis, all that billionaire rock stars and celebrities are searching for, is to be loved. Such a long route they have to take! And such a mistaken one too. Their stardom itself isolates them from the very people they once dreamed of being intimate with. They live in fear and anxiety and flee from their fans. The gates of heaven open into hell! Performing has become their lifeblood, for they know no other way of being loved. They feel unloved unless they keep proving it and re-proving it, not to the audience but to themselves by demonstrating before a large crowd their lovableness! As Elton John once admitted, "Even if I had only one finger left, I would play (the piano) for you just to be loved." Said Oscar winning British actor Sir Anthony Hopkins when he recently announced to the world his decision to quit acting, "To hell with this stupid show business. Everything was a fake."

No. Overblown riches or fame usually become an obstruction to the experience of love. The sight of material opulence seduces the unwitting, star struck adolescent to the false philosophy that an increase in quantity of wealth, possessions, acquaintances and fans means a corresponding increase in happiness. Thus he or she embarks on a career many later regret: Elvis Presley, Marilyn Monroe, Chris Farley, Mike Boorda, Vincent Foster....

It is said that the closest thing to the happiness of God, is your mother's love. But how long can you remain in her lap or hold her hand? How long will she remain with you in this ephemeral world? But God has bestowed humans with a great blessing – His love or the love of a God-communion Sadhu.

Those who offer profound love to God and His Sadhu have truly grasped the secret of eternal happiness. Mira offered profuse devotion to Shri Krishna. The paramhansas and devotees of Bhagwan Swaminarayan rejoiced in divine bliss through their love and devotion for Him.

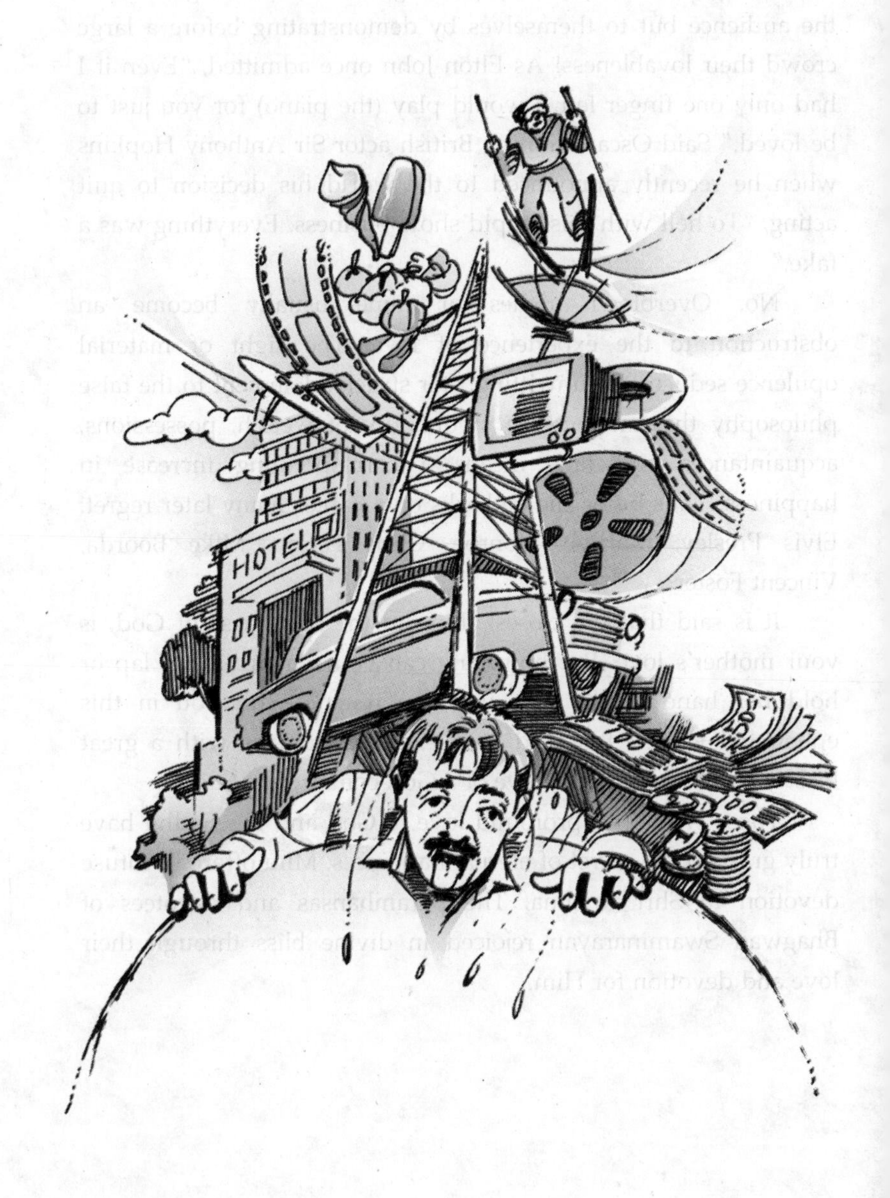
HOTEL

WHO IS THE HAPPIEST OF THEM ALL?

Human beings are the happiest creatures on this earth. He (and she) have the highest intelligence of all life-forms and possesses a wealth of scientific gadgetry to make his and her life simple, easy and pleasurable: jet planes, comfortable cars, HDTVs, digital cameras, internet mobile phones, designer clothes, fast food, delicious drinks – and so much more!

Sometimes a human being can become so happy he or she even commits suicide. No other creature has been known to do this. Amongst the happiest people in the world, as you probably know, are the Americans. America has one of the highest number of suicides – about 560 per week – a total of 30,000 per year. The Japanese follow closely behind with 26,000 suicides per year and are followed in turn by the French and Germans who have nearly 13,000 suicides per year.

That's not all. Sometimes, man's happiness turns to ecstasy – and he commits murder. As a part of the "American Dream" package, without any extra costs attached, 403 murders are committed every week in America – nearly 21,000 murders per year. The Brazilians follow with approximately 10,000 murders per year, and the French and Germans follow with 2,600 murders per year.

The despotic rulers of the past were far more terrifying. Hitler, for example, ordered the extermination of all Jews in Germany: approximately 6 million were gassed, buried alive or shot at his whim. And Mao (Zedong) Tse-tung, leader of the Chinese government between 1949 and 1965, was even more cruel than Hitler. He ordered the massacre of 26.3 million of his own countrymen.

And how can we forget the Russians? Vladimir Lenin, Joseph Stalin and Nikita Khruschchev were bent on making others joyful. Under their regime from 1917 to 1959, they ordered the slaughter of 66.7 million of their fellow men.

Though in the year 2001, man is not as happy as he used to be, there are still many points: everyday, all over the world there are millions of racial attacks, burglaries, thefts and assaults. Thousands are being killed in wars, terrorist attacks and family feuds. Millions of parents live in old people's homes and millions of children live in orphanages because neither care a dime for each other.

No!!! Man is not an happy animal. He is probably the most wretched and miserable of all God's creatures. If he was happy and satisfied, he would never take his own or somebody else's life. Nor would he be jealous of others or compete with the people next door and his greed for more and more wealth, prestige and power would sublimate into thoughts of philanthropy and altruism.

There are perhaps very few people who are totally fulfiled in their hearts, desiring no more than they already have. Nearly every human being suffers some sort of loss or misery – a job redundancy, breach of trust, embezzlement, disobedient child, poor examination results, bills, debts, poor health or bereavement. To join the ranks of the truly happy and to justify his position as God's Crown creation, all peoples of the world need to count their blessings instead – even if those blessings are in common with everybody else. These blessings include the commonest of things such as having eyes, a complete body, good health, loving parents, shoes and clothes to wear, food and water to eat, drink and bathe, friends and simply being alive. Try it! Take a pen and paper and begin writing down your blessings. Go over them everyday. You'll be surprised to discover yourselves blessed with a thousand benedictions and goodies you never realized were there.

TIME...

BREVITY OF LIFE

A man jumped off the 114th story of the Empire State Building in New York City claiming that he would survive the fall. As he hurtled by each floor people inside could hear him say, "So far so good! So far so good!"

It is unfortunate that many people think they're going to live forever - only awakening to their mortality after the age of 45 when arthritis and serious debilitating illnesses such as heart disease set in. It is usually only then that people start wondering what life is all about - whether they have missed something, whether any of the things they had really strived for and achieved were really worth it. The recent earthquake at Gujarat awakened millions of people to the intrinsic hollowness of life's achievements. In December 1997, a Silk Air Boeing 737-300 suddenly exploded in midair. All 104 passengers aboard died in the disaster. The irony was that a famous book author who was aboard the flight - Bonnie Hicks - had just written an article in the Sunday Times at Singapore on the recent death of her grandmother. "The brevity of life cannot be over emphasized," she wrote. "I cannot take for granted that time is on my side, because it is not. Granny's death has put that sharply into focus." Shortly after, Bonny Hicks boarded the ill-fated Silk Air flight! Such incidents happen everywhere. No one is truly safe - however advanced the technology and safety procedures being taken. For instance, the Alliance Airlines crash in India took the lives of nearly 60 people. Their deaths were blamed on the age of the plane or a failing of the pilot or airport staff to adhere to basic safety procedures. Then, a few days later, the most advanced commercial aircraft in the world with the most stringent of safety regulations - Concorde - caught fire and crashed into a hotel in France, killing all of its 113 millionaire passengers! What do we conclude? At billionaire fashion designer Gianni Versace's funeral, Princess Diana cried profusely. A few days later, she herself died in a terrible car accident. At the hospital, doctors tried for two hours to save her life. But her time was up. Surrounded by the most advanced medical facilities in the world or even a thousand doctors, one will still have to go. By hook or by crook everybody has to go. Even a doctor has to go. This is the way of the universe. The Romans thought their empire was invincible, therefore they named it *Roma Eterna* - "Eternal Rome". But today it exists no more. The British built New Delhi thinking they would be here for another thousand years. But they had to leave and return home. Says Bhagwan Swaminarayan, "One day even this Earth shall be no longer. The Sun will be no longer; nor will there be a record that they ever existed." This is the sealed fate of absolutely everything in the universe. In fact one day, even the universe will be no longer.

But, if one has lead a life of goodness and philanthropy, one has no need to fear death. In fact, one can welcome it, because one will be making a transition to a higher, eternal place in God's lap. We only pass through this place once, so why not make it as pleasant as we can for others so that they will remember us for years afterwards? And what have we to lose in doing so? We brought nothing with us when we came, and we won't take a single penny with us when we leave. In fact, we will all leave a little extra behind. An ill-mannered and selfish person refused to vacate a seat for a disabled traveler aboard a bus. When the ill-natured passenger finally disembarked, the conductor called behind him, "Sir, you've left something behind." "What?" asked the man turning around. "A bad impression," replied the conductor.

Said Sant Kabir, "When you were born, you cried and the world rejoiced. Live your life in such a manner that when you die, the world cries and you rejoice."

SANCTITY OF TIME

Time. So effervescent. So fleeting. So priceless. It just gets more and more precious for everyone. Why? Because everything is at its mercy – like the falling orange-peel finding itself aloft in the air and thinking to itself, "Good, provided it lasts."

It won't. Time is a commodity so limited that people are prepared to spend thousands of dollars per hour learning how to save it. But the truth is Time can never be saved. It must be spent. No dam can be built across the flowing rivers of Time. Neither can Time be irrigated from these rivers. All that can be done is to use it wisely. Not a moment should be taken for granted. In a famous non-fiction video-release called *Faces of Death,* a real, condemned serial murderer was shown being escorted by prison wardens at death row in the U.S. towards a room where he was to be executed. The harsh, echoing footsteps of the wardens can be heard poignantly. The sweat pouring down the prisoner's face is shown close-up. He is then bound to a chair in a small room with no windows. He is to die through gassing. Deadly fumes begin to descend from above. The terrified prisoner takes a deep breath in desperation. "That won't help," says the video commentator.

Frightening, huh? It is. Particularly for those who have not used their time usefully. There was a telling message on a gravestone: "I expected this - but not so soon!" It's always too soon for those who have not been able to spend their time well.

Time is very much like money: what you buy with it is up to you. If you choose, you can spend all your time slaving at the office. Or you can spend it all at the discos, cinemas or watching television. But unlike money and material things, Time is non-refundable. You may return a fur coat and retrieve your money. You may return a watch, camera or pack of biscuits for a refund if you are dissatisfied with the product. But you can't get a refund on Time. You can't get your life back at the time of your death. Not a second of it.

How, where and upon what, then, should a person spend his or her priceless, precious time? Isn't it OK to just spend it where almost every other person does? Where the popular film, music and sport's icons beckon us - eating, drinking, smoking, partying, disco dancing, wearing expensive clothes, buying expensive cars or just working like workaholics at the office from 9 a.m. to 10 p.m.? Who will guide us wisely in reply to this vexing question?

Truth lies on the lips of dying men. The so-called living actually live little. Their eyes are wide open, but they see less than the half-open eyes of a person on his deathbed. It is at those last moments that our eyes open widest. Sadly and ironically, wisdom dawns at the sunset of life.

Ask any dying person - a parent, friend, relative or even a person unknown to you where you should spend your Time. All will tell you: balance your work with family, friends, health and self. Spend more time on family, good books, meditation and prayers. Do more social work; do something for the citizens of tomorrow. Or ask yourself the question, "If I was given a chance to live my life over again, how would I live it?" Then start doing that. Another method: Always remember the Sanctity of Time. It is a gift from God. Do not squander it. Time is a gift God has given all His creatures. But human beings have been given the most quality time. Trees have the most quantitatively – thousands of years in some species. But so what? Would you rather be a tree, beast of burden or a human being? Decide.

Now go. You have no time to waste! Utilize every moment wisely. The stop-clock is ticking. You are running shorter and shorter of fuel; shorter and shorter of time. And your workload seems to be increasing day by day.

YOUR LIFE BUDGET

The best of countries and corporations are so because they have the best of budgets. It is but natural therefore, that many people are concerned about our local, national budget. But if they spent as much time worrying about their domestic budget as they did about the national one, the world would be a far better place. People remain glued to their TV sets for hours listening to the budget speech. They spend even more time criticizing it afterwards. But very few focus inwards to analyze the very poor way in which they have budgeted their own hard-earned money! Many continue to spend well beyond their income, inviting debts and sometimes bankruptcy. Bhagwan Swaminarayan has advised in His *Shikshapatri*, "One should keep a daily record of one's expenditure and income and should always live within one's means…and all - including the poor - should give something to charity." This is practical, grassroots budgeting.

Still fewer people have shaped a life budget for themselves. A life budget includes committing time to self, family, society and God. The lives of those who do this become richer - not just financially - but also socially and spiritually. Just as a country's budget must be well balanced for its economy to be healthy, so too does life have to be well balanced for it to be lived fruitfully.

Many corporate executives - like single-minded one-eyed cyclopes - invest all their time and effort in pursuing their careers and climbing the professional ladder. When they reach the summit however, most realize it wasn't worth the toil. They discover that the victory is empty and that they won it at an irreparable loss to their health, family and psyche: obesity, heart disease and fatigue on the physiological front; separated spouse, estranged children and uncared for parents on the familial front; frustration, depression and stress on the physio-psychological front. In US, Canada, China and Japan, this phenomenon has resulted in a tragic burgeoning of suicides and cardiovascular and cancer related deaths. The Royal Bank of Canada devoted one of its monthly letters to this problem with the title *Let's Slow Down.* "We are victims of mounting tension," it enunciated. "We have difficulty relaxing: we are not living fully."

For many in India too, life has become similar - like going downhill in a truck without brakes. Indians must awake. The World Health Organization (WHO) predicts that stress will be the number one killer in the world by 2020. And stress is usually nothing more than an individual's failure to balance his or her lifestyle. Living healthily and fully requires one to maintain regular food habits and diet; regular exercise and rest; spending time with family; working for charity and spending time in self-reflection, meditation and prayer.

There is only one way to survive overwork or burnout. Be brave and bail out! Or you will be a loser. The rat race of life only produces losers. It has no winners. Even if it does, the winner is still a rat. And usually a very large one. Asked a great sage to a prosperous king, "If you were about to die of thirst and starvation and someone offered you a glass of water and a loaf of bread in exchange for your wealth and kingdom, would you give them to him?" "Of course I would," replied the king. "Anybody would." "Then why," asked the sage, "have you wasted your entire life amassing all this land and wealth when they are worth no more to you than a glass of water and a loaf of bread?"

Consider deeply the value of your life. In the US, compensation for an injured knee is approximately $200,000. Then what to say for a damaged brain, injured eye, amputated leg, broken marriage or a mental breakdown? No price can be put on these things. What price, then, can we put on the entire, fully functioning human body?

Human life is priceless. God has bequeathed this limitless treasure trove to all. And as diversification is one of the secrets to successful investment, so is it the secret to a joyous and blessed life. Reach in to your soul, and out to your family, society and God. Budget well.

•

LIFE...

LOFTY PURPOSE OF HUMAN LIFE

A rich and learned man was crossing a large blue lake in a small boat. To pass his time, he asked the oarsman, "How much do you own?" "Only this boat and the clothes I'm wearing," came the reply. The rich man laughed. He asked another question, "Can you count to ten?" "No," came the answer again. The man of learning roared. Continuing the enquiry, he asked, "Do you know anything about business, politics, science, philosophy, dancing and the arts? Do you have any general knowledge whatsoever?" "None at all," replied the oarsman. The rich man guffawed and exclaimed, "Half of your life has gone in water!" Just then a great wave caused the boat to capsize and both of them tumbled into the lake. "Now may I ask you a question?" said the oarsman to the man of great intellect. "Go ahead," he replied. "Can you swim?" "No," came the response. "Then," observed the oarsman, "you will loose your whole life in water."

What is the purpose of our existence when whatever we do or achieve in life – like the rich and learned man crossing the lake –

counts for nothing in the final analysis? A great king approached a sage seated beneath a tree. Asked the sage, "O King! If you were in the desert and dying of thirst and a person offered you a glass of water in exchange for half of your kingdom, would you give it?" "Yes, of course – if it would save my life," replied the king. "And if later, you are dying of hunger," continued the sage, "and if somebody offered you a loaf of bread in return for the other half of your kingdom would you give it to him?" "Of course I would," replied the king." "Why, then, have you spent your whole life amassing all this land and wealth," the sage admonished, "when it is worth no more to you than a glass of water and a loaf of bread?"

Ultimately, nothing we gain in our lifetimes is worth more than a glass of water and a loaf of bread. Yet the fact remains that we exist – in all our pointless glory.

Is there, then, no special purpose to human existence? There is. And it stems not from our bodies but from our minds. Because of the depth and quality of his mind, man is a creature totally unlike any other amongst the one hundred million species around him. Other creatures have almost as much sense experience as man and in some areas, even more. But they lack the ability to think about and analyze their experiences. For instance, unlike Isaac Newton, they cannot ask the question "Why did the apple fall?" They cannot contemplate the puzzle, unlike Galileo, of whether the Sun revolves around the Earth or the Earth revolves around the Sun. They cannot probe the question "What is lightning?" unlike Benjamin Franklin nor can they conclude, "I think, therefore I am." unlike Rene Descartes.

This is what life is really about: observing, thinking and thoroughly understanding everything about ourselves and the universe. The joy is in comprehending. Concluded physicist Stephen Hawking in his best selling book *A Brief History of Time*, "Why is it that we and the universe exist? If we find the answer to that, it would be the ultimate triumph of human reason – for then we would know the mind of God."

This is the logical purpose of human life: the search for Truth, the whole Truth and nothing but the Truth. The Truth behind the culmination of all truths – physical, philosophical and psychological; the truth behind every word, concept or dream that may or may not be listed in all the dictionaries and encyclopaedias of the world; the truth about everything – including ourselves. If we can ask so seriously the question, "Why did the apple fall?" we certainly have to ask ourselves why the falling apple exists at all and the question of why we the observers of the apple exist in this universe too. We must acquire the answers to both these questions – "Apara" and "Para Vidya" say the Upanishads. Not a master of either; nor a jack of both. A Master of both. The ephemeral and the eternal. The mortal and the immortal. The soul and the Lord.

This is the lofty purpose of human life.

WHAT IS LIFE?

What is life? This is a question which has been discussed and debated by the most sublime minds of each century right back to the dawn of civilization.

"A life without introspection is not worth living," asserted Socrates around 400 BCE. "Survival of the fittest," said evolutionist Charles Darwin in his voluminous work *The Origin of Species* in the mid-1800s. "Crush the infamy!" wrote the French philosopher Voltaire in his effort to forestall the omnipotent and aberrant church in Europe during the late 1700s. "Give me freedom or give me death," said the Americans of the freedom movement. "We will fight till the last drop of blood of man and beast," said Winston Churchill to the British people at the onset of the Second

World War. "Quit India," said Mohandas Gandhi to the British Imperialists. "Because it is there," replied Edmund Hillary when asked why he scaled to the peak of Mount Everest. "In 10 years we will put a man on moon," said John F. Kennedy at the onset of his presidency. "Make love, not war," said the hippies of the 1960s.

A thousand slogans have been chanted across the continents, a thousand pledges, a thousand oaths, a thousand and one mottos.

Whose ideology is the correct one? Which maxim reflects the highest, most lofty truth? Which slogan can bear the test of Eternity? Are there any peaks to ascend higher than Everest? Are there any planets to voyage towards beyond the solar system? Are there any worlds beyond the universe? Are there any depths deeper than the ocean's, beyond the heart's, further than the mind's?

Socrates was forced to drink hemlock, Darwin's theory collapsed, the Church became more democratic, the blacks got their freedom, the British defeated Hitler, the Imperialists left India, Hillary scaled Everest, America put a man on the moon, ... What next? A thousand more slogans and goals? A thousand more efforts and journeys? A thousand more struggles, undertakings and fantasies?

Technology will continue to flourish day by day and man will eventually harness the energies of the universe for his own utility. Who knows? He might even encounter new life forms - intelligent life - befriend them, and, hopefully - strive for the common benefit of both species. But toppling one goal after another, realizing fantasy after fantasy, indulging in the heart's every desire, a thoughtful person finally asks the question: what is the end of all this? The physical eye perceives no bottom to this dark, infinite abyss. The heart experiences no peace, no tranquility in the spinning maze of events which surround it. Indulgence in the temptations of the flesh - the forbidden fruit - bring him or her only frustration, anxiousness and regret.

A million years in the future this will continue to be the fate of our super ultramodern descendents far away in their spaceships and space stations in intergalactic space or on new, blue worlds amongst the isolated stars.

Man has a head but no crown. He achieves, but wins no trophy. He outranks and outshines all God's creatures, but he remains unresplendent amongst his own kind.

He searches for the zenith, yearning for a climatic, eternal joy. But it evades his every advance, from every direction.

Where must man hunt if he wishes to fulfil this aspiration, this alluring, unrelenting dream?

Man has searched outwards enough. Now he must seek within. To the very core of his or her own existence, to our substratum of consciousness which has made all our materialistic pursuits and enterprises possible. To the stream of consciousness we experience within ourselves throughout our lives, tying together all the events of our physical existence like the silken string of an unfurling garland. Here, man and woman will meet their journey's end, the Omega point, a place of final resting and the dawn of a new realization of the existence of the divine self and the beautiful, blissful Lord within. Says Bhagwan Swaminarayan in His Vachanamrut sermons: "The human soul perpetually peers outward towards mundane objects of the five senses, but he never looks inwards to see himself. Such a soul is the most ignorant and wretched of all."

Socrates wins.

RELIGION...

ARE RELIGIOUS PEOPLE SOCIAL MISFITS?

The materialist often views a religious person as unsociable, dogmatic and lacking in intellectual insight. The "freak" refuses to drink or smoke, prays before eating, frowns at the free mixing of the sexes and is superstitious, impractical and way behind the times.

If, for instance, he achieves a prominent position somewhere, he is regarded as abnormal and a nuisance to those around him because he refuses to take bribes! In schools and colleges, some students wear conspicuous religious marks on their forehead and their classmates take pride and joy in insulting and degrading them. Sometimes he (or she) may even be physically attacked for his religious beliefs. Sadly, occasionally, an allegedly religious person takes to the streets in an act of violence himself.

On all the above occasions, whether the religious person remains quiet or whether he speaks out, society at large takes him to be a social misfit.

The role of a religious person is not easy. He has to find a path which allows him to follow his beliefs in an environment that is constantly trying to pull him down. The mundane person, in comparison, is a social chameleon who incessantly changes his colour to match his surroundings. In a second, he can turn from capitalist into communist, friend into foe, Jekyll into Hyde. He has no principles, beliefs or goals except those which are conducive to his crude, sensual inclinations. He flies the flag not of his country, but of his customer. He sings the praises not of his wife and family but of his sports heroes. He sings the hymns not of his Creator but the songs of a film or play. These are the characteristics of the so-called "well-behaved" citizen.

"Normality" is equated with goodness and "unusualness" is equated with ignorance. In such an environment, it becomes very difficult for a religious person to win – particularly if he or she is a child.

But the religious social misfit knows in his soul that one day, the world will turn to his or her way of thinking. He or she sees everybody as essentially spiritual, but they have become sensual – rather akin to the proverbial lion-cub, which by mistake, joined a flock of sheep and goats. The religious person understands that though he may be a social misfit, others are misfits of a more serious kind. They are spiritual misfits. They do not fit into the wider, more important, spiritual scheme of things. This larger context has been completely missed by them, due to their keyhole perspective of the world.

The more we broaden our horizons – even on the physical level – the more spiritual we become! It is only when we narrow ourselves and our horizons, that we become mundane. The awareness of the infinite Cosmos and its miniature parallel – the human body – and the realization that everything consists of pure energy – bring about feelings of profound spirituality. This is why great scientists of the past, such as Albert Einstein, were awoken to a deep sense of mysticism.

On his return to Earth, astronaut Rakesh Sharma (who was the first Indian in space) described how he felt when he saw our wonderful globe suspended in infinite space. "Our planet looked so beautiful! And I just couldn't believe people were fighting down there."

It is well known that astronauts such as those who went to the moon, when they retire, very often become priests! Russian physicist Andrei Linde, whose brilliant contribution to science in *The New Inflationary Theory* predicts that the universe is actually billions of times larger than discernable through our telescopes, openly espouses mysticism and publicly expresses personal remorse about his career, "I'm depressed when I think I will die like a physicist," he says.

Please take a moment and answer these questions for yourselves: if the whole world is blind, should you poke out your eyes or should you try to lead the way? If the whole world is lame, do you sever your legs or do you attempt to carry as many people as you can? And, if the whole world is insane, do you discard your intellect, or do you preserve your wisdom and strive to enlighten as many souls as possible?

Today, everyone is a misfit. Your answers to the above questions will reveal to you which one you are – social or spiritual!

UNITY IN DIVERSITY

The world around us everywhere spills over with a cascade of colours, a suffusion of scents and a symphony of sounds. All about us we witness countless life forms – plants, insects, birds, fish and mammals. Yet there exists an estimated 10 to 100 million life forms still to be classified and catalogued. The task will take all our diligent scientists about 5,000 years to complete!

Diversity is what makes our world rich. It gives our existence depth and our perspective ever broadening horizons. Diversity has bequeathed us a thousand languages, as many cultures, histories and legends. Diametrically opposed thinking has led to progressive philosophies from Thales to Plato to Kant. It has revealed successive truths in science from Newton to Einstein to Bohr. Diversity leads us from truth to truth, expanding our reach to ever increasing ranges. Today, we know roughly how the universe was created, how stars function and what lies below the ocean waves. All around the world, a galaxy of scientists have contributed to the renaissance of pragmatic, sensible thinking and living.

But it is not enough. Man needs to know more. What is the universe for? What is life all about? Life is so fragile, death so near. Despite the kaleidoscope of attractions the world presents, time and death will cancel it all. The world remains silent on these issues – love, pain, bereavement and the overwhelming forces of nature – droughts, plagues, cyclones and earthquakes. Here, scientific answers fail to console. The injured heart and tormented mind need a deeper answer and the answer must have meaning. The scientific answer "that's just the way the universe is" just won't do. Said the eminent physicist Erwin Schrodinger, "The scientific picture of the real world around me is very deficient. It gives me a lot of factual information, puts all our experience in a magnificently consistent order, but it is ghastly silent about all and sundry that is really dear to our heart, that really matters to us." Says the celebrated physicist Stephen Hawking in his best selling book *A Brief History of Time*, "Why is it that we and the universe exist? If we find the answer to that, it would be the ultimate triumph of human reason – for then we would know the mind of God."

Every religion in the world is a laboratory to seek, discover and understand the 'mind of God'. Each religion represents the institution which formed around its early teachers and disciples. Till the search for God continues, no credible religion in the world needs to be closed down. No angle of approach need be rejected; no methodology of worship overturned. A multipronged, holistic approach through the sincere efforts of all the religions will ultimately bring irrefutable results from one religion or another.

Neither should any attempt be made to unify the world's religions. Trying to combine the lot to form a type of 'super-religion' makes as much sense as trying to merge the Arts, Commerce and Science Institutes into a single class! Different people have different ideas, preferences and aptitudes. They can flourish only in that particular arena. It's where they can be their best, contribute their most. Every religion has a unique historical, social, cultural and spiritual context. Trying to unify all the religions would probably be a disaster. You cannot create a 'supercar' by building it from a mixture of parts taken from Rolls Royces, Mercedes, BMWs and Lincolns! A hotchpotch car probably wouldn't even start, and if it did, any passenger had better get out quickly - it would be a death trap. Similarly, a mixture of religions would contradict itself in almost every area and would never be a success.

Let each man continue his own way. Let each religion blossom its own way. Let each religion be respected and acknowledged for the virtues they embody. Together, the religions of the world can be like a garland of mixed flowers - a cocktail of scents and aromas and a necklace of spangling colours hugging the hemispheres of our precious blue and green planet.

13

FACT OR SUPERSTITION?

A man went to an astrologer to check his horoscope. After peering at the calculations carefully, the astrologer looked up and said to the anxious inquirer, "Sir, it appears that your future holds more horror than scope."

The stars, planets and eclipses. The black cats, owls and cows. The fluttering of an eyelid, a bout of hiccups, a dream. In this world, almost nothing is without a meaning or bereft of an interpretation. Many tie lemons and chillies to their doorways or vehicles to ward off evil spirits. Others wear exotic rings on their fingers and talismans around their necks. Abroad, people avoid walking on cracks in the pavement, or beneath a ladder or acquiring a flat on the 13th floor of a building. And for heaven's sake don't drop that mirror! If it breaks, it means seven years of bad luck!

Are these mere superstitions or is their some truth in any of this? People believe talismans and coloured stones have improved the quality of life. Others argue that if this *jantra-mantra* or hocus-pocus was true, there would be no need for governments around the world to maintain and build expensive armies and arsenals with nuclear warheads. All a leader need do is employ a good tantric and he'll create hell for his political enemies using just a few seeds of mung or by piercing a small doll replica of the enemy leader with pins. Yet, why don't we see such incidents occurring anywhere? Certainly, there are clear references to tantric procedures and practices in the Atharva Veda and Shiv Tantra scriptures showing that such powers do exist and can be honed into. But these are very difficult and ancient practices. How can people know them today? Could it be just by chance and coincidence that things seem to happen due to magical powers? In school we were taught a law which reigns above all the others in the universe, called Murphy's Law. It states categorically, "If anything can go wrong, it will!" Sooner or later, something goes wrong in almost everybody's life and you may conclude that your misfortunes were due to a tantric casting spells upon you when in fact your bad luck was due merely to complex and unforeseeable environmental, social or financial events such as the fall of the Nasdaq Index or simply because of some unwise decisions. Even mega-companies which were booming just six months ago like video site reel.com and online retailer amazon.com are today struggling for business. So are thousands of other dot.com companies. Is it because some tantric is working his powers on the e-commerce of the world? Personally, I think we create our own mindsets and then interpret our situation in a way that fulfils it. An old woman was throwing grains of rice around her house. "Why?" asked a neighbour. "To keep tigers away," she replied. "But there aren't any tigers around here," objected the neighbour. "Effective, isn't it?" said the old woman jubilantly.

Whatever the answer to this conundrum, one thing should be understood clearly: the greatest and most powerful of 'tantrics' is God. One who has deep and single-minded devotion to God need not fear tantrics or ill omens. Even if outwardly it appears some evil force is harming them, they themselves understand that what is happening is happening only because of the will of their Lord, to whom they have surrendered themselves. They refuse to surrender to tantrics and black magicians even if they are faced with death! For such devotees, God Himself becomes their surety and security. So if one day you find that someone has thrown mung seeds or placed a lemon in front of your doorstep, thank the person, collect the seeds together, wash them, boil them, offer them with love to the deity and have a hearty meal. Or else give them to some poor person or donate them at the mandir. Keep your faith in God firm and continue on your way unruffled. Even if the tantric's powers are genuine, they will not work on you – in fact, it will be the tantric who better watch out. It all just may backfire on him.

$(x+y)^2 = x^2+2xy+y^2$
$Na_2HPO_4 \rightleftharpoons 2Na^+ + HPO_4^{2-}$
$C_6H_{12}O_6+6O_2 \rightarrow 6Co_2+12H_2O+38ATP$
$F = Gm1m2/r^2$
$\frac{d(x+y^2)}{dy} = 2x+1$

ARE SCIENCE AND RELIGION ONE?

Does God exist? If He does, where is He? Very few people in the past have claimed to have seen Him, and mysteriously He hasn't at all revealed Himself to the modern world in such a way that we can verify His existence scientifically. Is there any real justification for believing in such a God? Are there any truly unshakeable grounds for putting our faith in a few obscure individuals of antiquity who claim to have witnessed Him? To many, in particular those of the scientific breed, the faith of the masses is misplaced in religion and needs to be transferred to the empirical and "pragmatic" realm of science. Scientists claim they will one day be able to answer all the questions of the universe, its functioning and its creation without needing to appeal to a transcendental God, on the basis of the laws of nature.

Baloney! Many scientists seem to have completely overlooked the fact that even the existence of these so called "laws of nature" is itself a purely ad hoc assumption! Where do these laws reside? What are they made of? Why can't we see them? Where do they come from? Certainly, scientists have discovered mathematical regularities in the workings of the universe which allow them to make accurate predictions. But that is not at all the same as showing us the so called laws. The bottom line is, the existence of these laws as the governing force of the universe is equally as much an article of faith and metaphysical mystery as the existence of God! As physicist and Nobel Prize laureate Richard Feynman commented, "In the case of physics we have double trouble. We come upon these laws but there is no where for them. Yet we apply them to the universe so the problem of where the laws are is doubly confusing. These are philosophical questions I cannot answer."

So the puzzle remains who created this universe – God or natural law? If the answer is God, the next question is who created God? The conundrum, though quite humorous, continues ad infinitum and leads to no logical or practical solution, though an actual one must exist in reality.

Are we left with the famous "chicken/egg" enigma? Not quite. Though it is clear that the scientific theory is seriously flawed because it cannot accommodate the natural laws anywhere within the borders of the universe (and they cannot be positioned outside the universe, because in the opinion of science, there is no outside), the case for religion is very strong. The spiritual mind encounters no such enigmas at all. Contrary to the assumptions of science, the spiritual mind perceives that there is much more to the universe than meets the human eye, and that the acting of God's will has been construed by scientists to be the acting of natural laws. The laws are laws, certainly but they are not "natural" and they are not independent or without a source: their source and support is the conscious mind of God.

Still, unknown to many non-scientists – and, to the dismay of many "orthodox" scientists – resorting to some form of consciousness or another as the basic cause of all physical phenomena has been proven inescapable even from the brute atomic theories of quantum physics! Moreover, Templeton Prize winner physicist Paul Davies states that science also assumes the laws of nature to be "omniscient", "omnipotent" and "eternal". All of these attributes are precisely the same attributes the religious mind ascribes to God! Science, it seems has turned full circle. Whatever differences of opinion exist between the two schools of thought are mostly that of language and are of no greater (or lesser) consequence than the differences in theology which already exist between the philosophies of the world's religions.

But unlike the scientific mind, the spiritual mind requires no instruments other than itself to understand and acknowledge the Lord's existence. The religious person sees with inner vision – an intuitive capacity almost entirely absent in the pure empiricist. The eye of a telescope or microscope will never be enough to reveal God to the materialistic observer. Only the inner eye will.

Nevertheless, there is a marvelous central point of convergence for all the world's religions and science – the common belief in the existence of some sort of Supreme, Omnipotent and Conscious all-doer. That is enough for all to join hands and celebrate!

OPEN YOUR HEART TO GOD

Whether your allegiance is to science, philosophy, religion, a cult or even a superstition, a deep feeling and conviction persists that some sort of Higher Energy, Deeper Principle or Sovereign Power is at play in our universe – maintaining all the physical order we see around us. In fact, the conclusion is inescapable.

Call it 'Nature' or call it 'God'. It makes little difference. All believe in His existence. Sadhus, sannyasins and lay followers seek to achieve His direct experience through prayers, meditation, devotion, austerity and service. The world's top scientists are trying to glimpse His inner logic with the help of telescopes, microscopes and supercomputers. They have even pet named the theoretical baby they hope their investigations will eventually give birth to: *The Theory of Everything* or *TOE*. Quite appropriate. Said

Bhagwan Swaminarayan, "When I press my toe against this earth, the earth and millions of planets like it in the cosmos undulate in their positions." Yes, a toe – God's toe – is the answer to everything that happens in the universe!

On the moral front, belief in God's existence has become indispensable for the effective functioning of human civilization. The material universe taken alone cannot provide us with the ethics required for orderly, amenable life – as evolutionist Charles Darwin himself lamented. The universe would simply decree, "survival of the strongest, most devious and scheming animal." Gross survival would be the only goodness. Death would be the only evil. There would be absolutely no rules. Amassing wealth, power and status would be the only virtue. Humility, economy, equality, charity and sacrifice would be the only sins. As the illustrious German philosopher Immanuel Kant clearly demonstrated in his *Moral Argument,* without God's existence or Life after Death, nothing would matter: there could exist no such thing as right or wrong. If you plunder a village or ransack a city or embezzle someone's money and build yourself a palace, you will have done nothing immoral. This is the perverse equation of the universe when bereft of a spiritual input. It is the formula followed by Hitlers, hit men and hoodlums. What is it to be, asks Kant – murder and theft are correct or ethics and morality are correct? Even the most diehard atheist would opt for morality. Quipped French deist and philosopher Voltaire, "If God did not exist, it would be necessary to invent Him."

But there are also tremendous scientific grounds for the belief in a supreme creator. For example the "Big Bang" explosion which created the universe was such a harmonious and coordinated event that it doesn't qualify as a true explosion at all. It was more of a revelation – like the delicate and sequenced unfolding of a rose bud in the morning. "In fact," says British physicist Roger Penrose, "the chances of the universe unfolding as it has, together with its ability to evolve and sustain life are 10^{60} to 1 against!" (10^{60} means 1 followed by 60 zeros).

Even more fabulously, at the other end of the spectrum, God's unmistakable hallmark can be discerned in life's basic building block: the DNA molecule. Its marvelous design, magnificent functioning and superb self-reproducing capacity are nothing short of miraculous. The chances of this DNA appearing by chance is $10^{40,000}$ to 1 against, said late physicist Fred Hoyle and colleague Chandra Wikramsinghe. ($10^{40,000}$ means 1 followed by 40,000 zeros). To negate God is to negate oneself; one's own existence.

Go on. Take a close look around you. Still can't see anything? Then maybe you need to open your eyes a little wider. Or maybe you need to open your heart. The intellect can only analyze, divide and dissect. The heart can feel, synthesize and unify.

RELIGION, RITUALS AND RATIONALISTS

"Religions, rituals and temples are a total waste of time and money," say the so-called rationalists. Such allegations are hardly justified or intelligent. People who speak this way usually lack the most basic knowledge of culture, psychology, social psychology, preservation of history, heritage and religious beliefs. Said Huston Smith in his influential book *The Religions of Man*, "Let just one generation fall down in its job of passing on the wisdom of the fathers and the human venture will be set back half a million years."

Contrary to what some people think, rituals are not synonymous with religion, though they are inseparable. Rituals represent the bark of a tree. The tree cannot survive long without its bark. Neither can any religion or society without its rituals. Rituals are gestures and symbols of social, political and religious events of the distant past and are also useful in teaching abstract ideas and concepts. For instance the whole of mathematics is nothing but ritualistic procedures for manipulating symbols in accordance with abstract algorithms. Counting and subtracting beads on an abacus is also nothing but a ritual. But without going through this process, it would be difficult for people to learn to count even to one hundred! Rituals also give form to difficult and abstract philosophical ideas, thus making them easily understandable and accessible to the masses. For instance the waving of the *arti* represents the spiritual sound of the abstract AUM - which in turn represents the greatness of the divine and transcendental God.

Even the hardheaded, no nonsense military is full of rituals! Why do soldiers and other country servicemen spend so much

time and energy polishing their buttons and boots and marching up and down an empty compound? Yet when a *pujari* wipes a *murti* of God with a cloth to remove dust and circumambulates around the deity with devotion (*pradakshina*), people scream "Ritualism!" When the national flag is hoisted into the air, people stand to attention. When a flag is raised to God and flutters over a mandir, people shout "Ritualism!" When a person wears flashy clothes to a party or wedding, shaves and gets a haircut, people praise him. If a person shaves his head and wears simple clothes upon the death of a loved one, people cry out "Ritualism!"

All religions and nations have their rituals. Intelligent leaders know the value of rituals. Without them, not only would we forget the past 500,000 years of human history and its lessons, we would also miss celebrating the joys of the present. What would a wedding day be without the feast and firecrackers? What would a birthday be without the candles and songs? What would our Earth be, bereft of festivals, commemorations and observances? Rituals are our riches. To renounce them would be to invite cultural poverty and religious ignorance. Bhagwan Swaminarayan explains in His Vachanamrut sermons that places of worship need to be constructed to bequeath future generations the experience and wisdom of their founders through a standardized procedure of worship, service, austerity and meditation - much as in the method of mathematical algorithms.

Rituals also serve to prevent social disintegration by bringing thousands of people together with a spirit of oneness, which is hard to come by while people are going about their individual daily routines. Thus, as an almost complete and holistic nourishment, rituals educate, coordinate and sublimate our lives.

In fact the whole of human history has been that of rituals. Those who repudiate them should think about what they wish should happen to their bodies after their death. Do they wish to be buried or cremated? Or do they want their bodies to be left lying around for dogs and crows to eat or simply collected by the municipality and discarded at a dump like they do with animals? Remember, burials and cremations are rituals too! Rituals are what make and keep us humans civilized and a plane above the beasts. A priest and his friend sat down together for dinner at a restaurant. The priest began to pray first whilst the other began to eat immediately. With his mouth still full of food, he finally said to the priest, "I don't bother praying. I eat right away." "Even my dog does that," replied the priest. Now you must choose – rituals or no rituals!

SPIRITUAL POTENTIAL

The laws of the spiritual transcend and bypass those of the material. Souls which have actualized their divine potential are able to leave or enter their physical bodies at will or even enter something inanimate like a stone or piece of wood and make it walk or talk as though it were alive! This is not all. The Shrimad Bhagwat says, "The wise can see the whole universe with their eyes perfected in yoga." If they so desire, explains Bhagwan Swaminarayan going a step further, they can even reach out with their physical arms and take into their hands any object from any place in the universe! Such statements are sometimes hard to digest for the uninitiated and unendowed, much as space travel or flying would have been incomprehensible to even the most learned and broadminded person just two hundred years ago. But the undeniable fact of these claims concerning the power of the soul can be proven today from their mind boggling scientific insight in an age when people still believed the earth was flat. An example: Bhagwan Swaminarayan clearly reveals in one of his sermons that the size of the solar system is fifty *crore yojans*. This translates into precisely 3.5 billion miles: the average distance from the sun to the solar system's outer most planet – Pluto. But at that time Pluto hadn't even been discovered! How did Bhagwan Swaminarayan know of its existence and its distance?

And does not all history speak? Have not all the great saints of our Earth performed extraordinary feats during their periodic but fleeting stays in our midst? Certainly, not even the best of magicians today have yet been able to create an illusion of lifting an entire mountain on the tip of their index finger or creating nine hundred thousand exact clone copies of themselves and then embracing an audience of nine hundred thousand individuals personally and simultaneously. These are just some of the miracles that our forefathers have recorded in the history of their experiences. This is not to say there have never been con artists and crooks who cheated the people. Only to say you can't fool all the people, all of the time. Fakes don't hang around long after performing their "miraculous" stunts to gather a following – they have to make a quick getaway before people realize they've been duped. The tricksters' purpose was to earn quick cash to fill their bellies. In contrast, truly spiritual people do not flee; they believe in the spiritual message they preach and have chosen a life of sensual abstinence, self denial, chastity and charity. They never ask for anything for themselves. They don't need to. They are already monarchs of the universe.

Only rarely are saints born saints. Usually, they're born just like other human beings with many human deficiencies or limitations. However, through untiring practice of spiritual disciplines under the guidance of a spiritual Master, they burst through their human barriers and limits and enter into the illimitable world of the Divine. Everyone – male and female – can do it if they try hard enough. But even if this infinite spiritual domain remains beyond the reach of the seeker, his or her personal, social and spiritual life will benefit enormously: total peace of mind, contentedness, stresslessness, clearer thinking, stronger memory, improved concentration, healthier body, and a more positive and confident outlook on life.

Here are the techniques and disciplines required for developing one's spiritual potential: Self-Suggestion, Visualization, Self-Restraint, Chastity, Austerity, Meditation, Yoga, Vegetarian Diet, Abstinence from Smoking and Alcohol, Silence of Speech, Prayer, Contemplation, Introspection, Service to Man, Guru and God. Most people may not be in a position to practice and perfect all the above techniques and methods. But those who become totally accomplished in even one of them and in particular service to a Guru who himself is accomplished in all the qualities and virtues listed above, are well on the path to fully actualizing their spiritual potential.

THE MYTH ABOUT EVOLUTION

Suppose you are walking along a sandy beach. Your foot stumbles over something. You bend and pick it up. It is a rough and irregular rock. Without much thought you would probably throw it back. But suppose you are the first human being to be walking on a distant planet orbiting another star at the far end of our galaxy. Again, you stumble over something. You pick it up. It's a digital watch! The discovery would be the most exciting event in human history because the watch could not conceivably have been created by some fluke of nature, like the rock back on Earth. The digital watch contains too much design! We know that such design can only be achieved through deliberate and purposeful manipulation of metals and minerals by intelligent beings!

This analogy is known as the Argument for Design, first advanced by the Natural Theologist, William Paley (1743-1805) to demonstrate the existence of God as the creator of our beautiful and orderly Universe and its meticulous governing laws. The glorious and majestic structure of the large-scale universe – the dynamics of planetary orbits around the sun and the sun's orbit around the centre of the galaxy, are also examples of exquisite, purposeful design.

The "Big Bang" explosion, which created the universe in the first place, is another example. Explosions are chaotic affairs. The Big Bang, however, was as harmonious and as coordinated as a world class orchestra! What are the mathematical probabilities of such an explosion occurring by chance? Answer: 10^{60} to one against. Roger Penrose of Oxford University draws an analogy to this exceedingly improbable event. Suppose we place a target just one foot wide, right at the far extreme end of the universe - say 15 billion light years away. (That's some 15 million, million, million miles away!) Then, you take random aim from Earth with a revolver specially loaded with bullets able to traverse that distance - fire - and hit the bull's eye! That is how precisely coordinated the Big Bang explosion was!

But the most fabulous proof of God's handiwork lies not in the galaxies or the stars, but in our own selves! Life, it turns out, and above all, human life, is an almost impossible occurrence. The basic building block of life is known as DNA. The miracle seems to lie not just in its amazing intricacy but also in its ability to self-replicate in ingenious combinations and fold and unfold only at the right moment.

The big question is: how did the complex DNA molecule come to exist? Evolutionists - for want of another idea - have pressed a theory of chance. It goes like this: by fortuitous coincidence, there came to exist on earth an ocean of primeval "organic soup" which contained simple molecules of carbon and hydrogen. By pure chance again, over a period of one billion years these simple molecules of carbon and hydrogen, maybe with a little help from ultraviolet rays from the sun and lightning from the atmosphere, bumped and brushed into each other sufficient times to combine and form organic molecules such as sugar and amino acids. Then, again by fluke, every single one of these billions of chance interactions conspired positively rather than negatively to create the famed DNA molecule!

Is evolutionary theory even remotely credible even if we stretch our imagination and fantasies to their limit? Fred Hoyle, one of the most eminent scientists of our age, and his colleague Chandra Wickramsinghe, shake their heads. "The trouble is," says Hoyle, "that there are about 2000 enzymes, and the chance of obtaining them all in a random trial is only one part in $(10^{20})^{2000}$ = $10^{40,000}$ - an outrageously small probability that could not be faced even if the whole universe consisted of organic soup."

The theory of evolution is an insidious superstition of science and is at best highly speculative armchair philosophy. From the glorious myriad of spectacular sights and colours of the present day, through to the lingering sounds and echoes of a beautiful cosmic symphony played during the earliest moments of creation, we are incessantly forced to bear witness to the compelling and veritable evidence of a masterful and powerful Conscious Creator.

For those who are able to integrate both head and heart, the existence of God is not merely an idea or a belief. It is a wonderful, observable fact.

POWER OF PRAYER

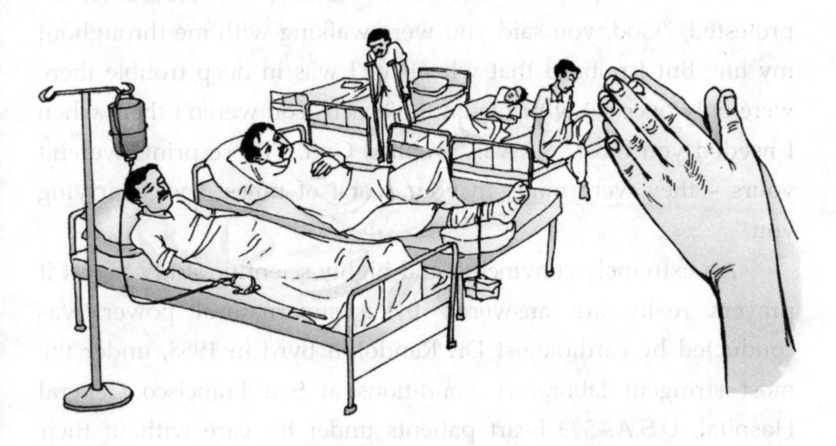

Once, a priest accidentally fell off a cliff. But as he plummeted towards his death he was luckily able to grasp hold of an old protruding tree root. Hanging precariously a thousand feet above the ground, he prayed aloud, "Please save me, O Lord!" For some time, there came no reply. Then, just as his energy was running out and his fingers were beginning to lose their grip on the root, the Lord called from the sky, "I will save you on one condition: first let go of the root." The priest thought for a while and then responded meekly, "Is anyone else up there?"

Millions of people pray every day. But many of them lack faith. They lack confidence and conviction. God, however, is infinitely graceful despite our lack of faith in Him. He continues to help us in our times of need, though we may not have the required insight, intelligence or spiritual inclination to discern or acknowledge the miracles that occur all around us every day of our lives. Once, after a devout man died, God showed him a video recording of his life. On one side of the picture there was also a vertical strip which showed a beach with two sets of footprints along it. "What does this show?" asked the man. "One set belongs to you and the second set belongs to me," answered God. "Throughout your entire life I was walking along with you." The man was pleased. But after viewing the recording, he protested, "God, you said you were walking with me throughout my life. But I noticed that whenever I was in deep trouble there were only once set of prints on the beach. You weren't there when I needed you most." "I was," replied God. "Those prints weren't yours – they were mine. In your worst of times, I was carrying you."

An extremely convincing and highly scientific study to test if prayers really are answered by a supernatural power was conducted by cardiologist Dr. Randolph Byrd in 1988, under the most stringent laboratory conditions at San Francisco General Hospital, U.S.A. 393 heart patients under his care without their knowing, were split into two groups. The names and medical condition of all the patients of one group were given to a prayer group who agreed to pray for them regularly. No such arrangement was made for patients in the other group. Ten months later, Dr. Byrd found that the health of the group that was being prayed for was twenty-one times better than those not being prayed for. Patients in the group being prayed for were also five times less likely to need heavy antibiotics and three times less likely to develop complications than the group not being prayed for! Said the eminent U.S. physician Dr. Larry Dossey, "If these results were brought about by medicine, they would have been heralded as a major breakthrough." Said another distinguished medical professional Dr. William Nolan, "If this is a valid study, we doctors ought to be writing on our prescriptions, 'Pray three times a day'." This is the now scientifically proven power of prayer. As Alfred Tennyson used to say, "More things are wrought by prayer than this world dreams of."

But what about the fact that God sometimes really doesn't

answer our prayers? Maybe it's because we're asking God for the wrong thing. Maybe we shouldn't always ask Him to move mountains. Maybe we should be asking Him for the courage to climb them! Maybe we should be asking more for internal strengths such as Determination, Patience, Will Power, Won't Power, Wisdom, Contentedness and Peace in our hearts. Maybe God isn't fulfiling our requests because he has already given us enough in our lives. Maybe the only prayer we need say in our life is, "Thank you, God." Maybe He wants us to start turning our attention away from ourselves and to begin praying for others. Prayers made for oneself – that is, for one's own body and material happiness – are of the lowest rank. Prayers for others are the most potent and noble – especially prayers for people not close to you or those you hardly know.

So tap into that Higher Source. It's a bonanza of riches, a windfall of inspiration and an ocean of blessings. You needn't go far. The gracious God is just a prayer away.

SELF...

BECOME YOURSELF!

"So, you want to become Sachin Tendulkar when you grow up?" I asked the 8-year-old boy as he walked past me swinging a cricket bat in his hand. We were on a house visit at a housing complex in Bandra, Mumbai. "No," he said scornfully. "I want to become myself." Congratulations to this wonderful boy who is truly one in a million. When so many other boys and girls similar to him in age and intelligence have made becoming someone else their life's dream, this child has realized that becoming oneself is all that one needs to do. Even after passing the age of forty or fifty, many still fail to realize that the people they are trying to resemble or imitate, are trying to resemble or imitate other people themselves!

Profound peace can only be experienced when one becomes oneself – and you will find that becoming yourself is all you need aspire for, despite your so-called outer deficiencies. These deficiencies are superficial. They are but symptomatic. Pursue yourself and you will expand and blossom, in time, into something more exquisite and beautiful than you ever imagined. You will find that it was only because you were trying to become someone else that you viewed yourself as deficient.

His Divine Holiness Yogiji Maharaj often narrated the incident of a young lion cub which, separated from its mother, roamed the forest absorbing like a sponge the characteristics of the sheep, squirrels and monkeys it was surrounded by. Some years later, the now youthful lion was spotted by a passing elderly lion. "Please don't kill me," pleaded the young lion. "I'm a small, helpless sheep and I have my whole life ahead of me." Amazed to hear these words from a member of its own kin, the elderly lion took the younger cat to a nearby waterhole. Gazing at its reflection with stupefaction, the young cat asked, "When did I turn into a lion?" "You always were one," replied the grown lion. "Only, you didn't know it." Thus the young lion roared and reentered the family of imperial animals.

So why doesn't everyone become a resplendent and majestic lion or lioness? Because they've covered themselves up with layer upon layer of thick mud and trash: fictitious and false personalities acquired through imitation and parroting of TV and film actors, actresses, musicians and dancers, bogus claims about one's education or income level, displaying wealth, clothes and jewellery beyond one's true level of earning and over-manipulation of one's appearance with the use of cosmetics and even facial surgery!

But how long will you continue to deceive yourself into believing you can become someone else? How long will you continue to finance with both your money and spirit the false facade you present to the people and to yourself? Instead, relieve yourself of the burden you have taken upon your shoulders. Throw it down and stand elevated. Be proud of who you are. You are not inferior to anyone. Discard following the public icons erroneously accepted as such just because they're rich and glamorous. Renounce chasing the shallow and half-baked. Pursue a career, yes. Pursue a personality, no. Pursue a mission, yes. Pursue an ambition, no. Live or die for truth, yes. Live or die for an illusion or myth, never.

And, just who is this person we should become – the individual we usually address as "me" or "I?" That person is the true you, the observer of your thoughts, your body and the world around you. You are the charioteer within your body; looking through your eyes, listening through your ears, tasting through your tongue and touching through your hands. You can never change, substitute or swap that true self of yours with anything else. And there is no need: you are eternal, immortal and divine. You are perfect as you are. And don't forget the even higher divinity within your self – the all-powerful, transcendent God. It is to His club we really belong and it is His qualities we should aspire to emulate: contentedness, innocence, mental purity, justice, forgiveness, love, care and compassion. Learn to adore and embrace these sublime and lofty characteristics of God and the need to create a false self will evaporate like a wisp of mist before the rising, morning Sun.

FINDING OURSELVES

In a devastating tragedy a man lost everything he had – his family, friends, wealth and status. As a result, however, he became aware of something exhilarating and uplifting. "I lost everything," he reflected excitedly, "but I found my self!"

The divine soul-self residing in our ephemeral bodies has been buried beneath umpteen shrouds of vanities: money, fame, status, power, the opposite sex, friends, colleagues, enemies, food, drink, addictions, make-up, jewellery, clothes, cars, computers – even the stars in the sky – in fact everything in the universe we attach ourselves to! In 1998, 947,000 females and 99,000 males in the U.S. underwent cosmetic surgery in a bid to improve their appearance. In the same year, 234 billion dollars were spent on cosmetic products worldwide!

But, the further out we wander into these wrappings, the more we lose contact with our centre, our essence. As a consequence we experience heightened levels of anxiety, anguish and emptiness. One meets with melancholy, dejection, and hopelessness. It is no surprise that 200,000 people in the U.S. and millions more around the world attempt suicide every year.

Individuals centred in their divine selves, however, are like people positioned in the eye of a hurricane: they encounter complete serenity. It is only when a person moves outwards, away from this centre, that he or she experiences buffeting – beset on all fronts by the perpetual onslaught of life's demands, pressures and adversities.

There is no need to blame anything, anybody or any event for your sufferings. Just return to your centre. That is where you are supposed to be. The people, events and environment may not be as they could be, but as far as your personal happiness is concerned they are not the source of your distress. You are. It is you who is mis-positioned. You are an umpire unwittingly chasing the ball at the boundary. You are a goalkeeper, mistakenly playing the role of attacker. You are a spectator who has inadvertently jumped into the boxing ring. Return to your seat. You are supposed to be an observer of your surroundings, not a part of them.

Life is really about retracing our steps and making a pilgrimage to our own nucleus. But because this inward trek is so difficult and abstract, man has chosen the more easily achievable goal of venturing to the moon, planets and stars. Or simply to the discotheque, cinema or sport's club. He has chosen to earn mountains of money, fame and status and to indulge in sensuousness as an easy alternative – the Primrose Path – rather than treading the unfamiliar and solitary path to his own glittering and effulgent centre stage.

The passage within is a stairway to eternal glamour and teems with colours, sights, sounds and tastes so tantalizing and exquisite that anything the outward world can offer appears as pittance in comparison! Like an Aladdin's cave, near its mouth there are rocks and dust, but deep within there lies priceless treasure – not emeralds, diamonds, gold and platinum – but substances far more precious, far more attractive and infinitely more enchanting. It is a magical world, where time stops, distances contract and expand, where actions merge, emerge and submerge. It is infinite; beyond the material world, yet the source of all its energies. It is an infinite ocean of light before which the luminescence of the entire universe appears as a mere flicker of a candle. The divine soul-self residing within the body is like a prodigal son of the ineffable Lord who Himself presides at the centre of each and every soul.

Anchor your lives in your soul and anchor your soul in God.

This is where the journey within culminates. And the path is not so long; the goal not so distant. In fact, promises Bhagwan Swaminarayan in his Vachanamrut sermons, "The inward path to God is so short that He and His divine abode are not even an atom's width away."

So close, yet so far. But repeated efforts under the guidance of a spiritual master are what lead to all great successes and they will also consummate in the greatest achievement of all – realisation of the transcendental, omnipotent God.

KNOW YOURSELF BEFORE YOU CAN KNOW LIFE

Scientists say the physical universe has no objective centre because the universe itself is expanding in all directions as a four dimensional space time continuum. Space time itself is in the process of expansion! Therefore there can be no fixed background or in built coordinate system against which to chart the ballooning cosmos and extrapolate even a hypothetical central point of origin.

Such may be the case from a technical point of view, but from a more pragmatic perspective, each and every living person is the centre of the universe, since for each person the universe exists only because he or she is there to observe it! This concept is so profound that even diehard scientists have conceded to two versions of it called the Strong Anthropic Principle (SAP) and the Participatory Anthropic Principle (PAP). The telescopes turn away from the receding cosmos and the arrows of all time passed and all futurity to come, train themselves upon you, the observer! The spokes of the great cosmic cartwheel emerge from you and merge back into you. You are the centre wherever you are, wherever you go.

But what are we at our very *core?* We are obviously much more than just our physical hands and legs, for if a person's limbs are amputated, his or her thinking ability will still remain whole: above all his other activities which are quite in common with other animals such as sleeping, eating and mating man is a thinking animal. And what a thinker! "The most powerful computer," say scientists John Barrow and Frank Tipler, "has a storage capacity and information processing rate between 10 and

1000 times less than that of a human being." Even the dimmest of human beings possess an information processing capacity 10 times greater than that of a Cray 2 computer. The IBM computer Deep Blue which defeated Gary Kasporov, regarded as probably the greatest chess player of all time, could perform an amazing 300 million computations a second. It's obvious that Mr. Kasparov was not using his whole brain! If even the dimmest human being was to use all of his or her information processing capacity Deep Blue would be a long way from defeating him or her and light years from defeating the brightest of human beings. And even then, two milestone theorems, Godel's Theorem and Searle's "Chinese Room", prove that mere information processing is not enough to divine knowledge. Self awareness or consciousness is a prerequisite.

So where does this leave us? For purely survival and propagation purposes, not only is the human being over endowed with information processing capacity, he or she also possesses consciousness. Why are we humans so over endowed with intelligence? What is the purpose? The answer is clear and inevitable. The purpose of human life is the search for Truth. The Truth. The Ultimate Truth.

But which Truth? The truth behind the culmination of all truths physical, philosophical and psychological; the truth behind every word, concept or dream that may or may not be listed in all the dictionaries and encyclopaedias of the world, the truth of everything, including ourselves. If we were to measure our success and prowess in terms of furthering our offspring, then animals and bacteria are far more successful than humans are. Then we would have to conclude that the human species is an inferior species compared to bacteria or that the goal of human life is different from that of animal life. The true purpose behind human life is not sensuality but spirituality. If we do not utilize this special and massive ability to contemplate and understand

Ultimate Truths, it means we have lived lives parallel to that of the other animals in the galaxy oblivious of everything but the here and now. In His Vachanamrut sermons, Bhagwan Swaminarayan states, "The human soul perpetually peers outwards towards objects of the senses, but the soul never looks inwards to see itself. Such souls are the most wretched of all."

Those who know this truth do not hanker after money nor do they drool over materialistic objects. Socrates was once in a market asking questions about various goods on sale. "I'm surprised to find you here,"said a friend. "Have you turned into a materialist?" "I have not the least desire to buy anything," replied Socrates. "I'm just amazed to see how many things I don't need in life."

THE SCIENTIFIC SEARCH FOR THE SOUL

Erwin Schrodinger, the father of Quantum-Wave Mechanics and one of the most eminent scientists who ever lived, declared, "The one and only task of science is to answer the one philosophical question: 'Who Are We?'" In the Kathopanishad, Nachiketa unremittingly requests Yamaraja, "Please give me knowledge of the Self."

Extrovert or introvert, for those who go deep into their respective fields of knowledge, a single, universal enigma incessantly and insistently surfaces at the centre of it: what is the nature of the observer of the field? And, for many scientists and intellectuals, the answer has remained a slippery eel indeed! In his book *The Astonishing Hypothesis – The Scientific Search for the Soul,* Nobel laureate Francis Crick sorely admits in the very opening sentence, "The mystery of consciousness ...at the present time...is far too difficult (to explain)." What is common with such armchair theoreticians is that none of them speak from experience – which is actually the essence of soul consciousness. They have to resort to reductionist and analytic methods of logic, which are inherently antithetical to the irreducible, indivisible and divine nature of the soul-self! Putting the final nail into the coffin of the reductionist method of these esteemed individuals, in 1931, the celebrated Austrian mathematician Kurt Godel demonstrated through his famous *Incompleteness Theorem* that the realm of pure logic and analysis can never be totally consistent or complete – it is fundamentally flawed!

Logic is of this world. Spiritual experience is of the other. Instead, it would be far better and immensely more sensible to simply shut one's eyes, turn within and delve deep. There, you come face-to-face with your divine self. You will have entered your inner shrine, beyond the arena of logic, into the illimitable and boundless magical world of the mystic. You will become aware of your own transcendental consciousness. This phenomenon of being conscious of one's own consciousness is the simplest testimony to one's spiritual identity.

Throughout history and even today, millions of people around the world are reporting to their doctors "out-of-body" or "near-death" experiences, where they have found themselves floating above their bodies during an operation or after a serious accident. Many doctors confirm the description of the operating theatres, etc. given by these patients and the medical discussions held while these patients were clinically unconscious. If we are merely our bodies, how could such out-of-body experiences occur? As Swami Vivekanand used to say, "We are not human beings having a spiritual experience, but spiritual beings having a human experience."

An experiment performed in 1979 by neuro-scientists Benjamin Libet and Bertram Feinstein has also unearthed impressive and compelling evidence for the independent existence of the soul. Measurements of the time taken for patients to react to an electrical stimulus given at various points on their skin, nerves and brain (with the use of electrodes) have shown that their consciousness of the stimulus is actually delayed for between one to one and a half seconds after the stimulus has been registered in his or her brain! One of the clear implications of this phenomenon, points out Professor Roger Penrose of the University of Oxford in his best selling book the *Emperor's New Mind,* is that consciousness is some sort of independent spectator residing within the human body witnessing a type of "action replay" of everything - rather as we witness a live cricket match being played abroad a fraction of a second after the event has taken place!

Bhagwan Swaminarayan explains in His Vachanamrut sermons that we are powerful monarchs of our own miniature kingdoms - our body, hands and feet. Our mind and senses - our eyes, ears, nose, tongue and skin - are our subjects. Our task is to become true masters of our mind and body rather than behaving as slaves. We need to learn to assert our sovereignty and guide them in such a way that they bring only betterment to this world and to ourselves in the next.

Even though one may know or understand little or nothing of this material and mundane world, if one has knowledge of the transcendent self, he or she is the wisest of all. As psychoanalyst Carl Jung said, "Who looks outwards, sleeps. Who looks inwards, awakes."

FAMILY...

A wealthy businessman arrived home as usual at 11 p.m. The excuse was different each night – unfinished work at the office, meeting with a customer, an important social function or event. "Dad," said his son one night. "How much money do you earn per hour?" "About $100. Why?" came the reply. His son pulled $200 out of his own pocket and placed it in his father's hand. "Will you give me an hour of your time?" he asked.

In today's age of minute-to-minute planning, deadlines, commitments and last minute alterations, parents are finding it increasingly difficult to find time for their children – to go out together for a stroll, picnic or shopping. What once used to be home has now turned into a hotel where members of the family come together to sleep. Isolated through conflicting schedules, sometimes members don't see each other for days! Parents arrive home long after their young children are asleep and children leave

BALANCING WORK WITH FAMILY

A wealthy businessman arrived home as usual at 11 p.m. The excuse was different each night - unfinished work at the office, meeting with a customer, an important social function or event. "Dad," said his son one night, "How much money do you earn per hour?" "About $100. Why?" came the reply. His son pulled $200 out of his own pocket and placed it in his father's hand. "Will you give me an hour of your time?" he asked.

In today's age of minute-to-minute planning, deadlines, commitments and last minute alterations, parents are finding it increasingly difficult to find time for their children - to go out together for a stroll, picnic or shopping. What once used to be home has now turned into a hotel where members of the family come together to sleep. Isolated through conflicting schedules, sometimes members don't see each other for days! Parents arrive home long after their young children are asleep and children leave for school long before their parents awake! Such a situation is potentially disastrous for both parents and their children. Parents miss the joys of playing with their own children and watching them grow up. Children miss the joy of a mother's cuddle and a father's playful pranks. Worse: the child fails to receive moral and ethical guidance which cannot be taught effectively elsewhere. "The primary responsibility of giving moral guidance," says His Holiness Pramukh Swami Maharaj, "lies with the parents." One mother can do more than one hundred good teachers.

A child has implicit faith in mum. Mum's the one who gives him or her everything – food, clothes, toys and protection from bullies. And dad looks after mum. This is why a child will believe almost anything a parent with love and affection teaches it. And when a child sees mum or dad faithfully practicing what they preach, the message goes straight to the deepest recesses of their souls where it remains embedded for the rest of their lives. They never forget those teachings.

A child, in fact, tends to distrust a message taught by someone relatively unknown.

No one can replace parents. They are the greatest teachers ever created. Nurturing is what they do best. No nanny, nurse or day keeper can replace them. Blood is always thicker than water. So it is crucial that parents realize their indispensability not only as providers for their children, but also as moral teachers and instructors for them. For that, parents first have to be visible. If they aren't, their children's impressionable minds will be indelibly stained and tarnished by what is visible: sex and violence on television; smoking and drugs in the alleys; loitering and truancy at school and colleges.

Out of sight out of mind. If they can't see you, you don't even exist! Sporadic appearances on your part merely give you sporadic existence. All the child has to do is wait for you to disappear again. Then he or she can go back to sleep, to the TV or worse. By age 16 the average child has watched 15,000 hours of TV and 150,000 violent scenes and 250,000 deaths! And surveys in the U.S. have revealed children from one-parent families are more prone to committing delinquent crimes! Is it any wonder?

Children need both parents to receive a healthy, balanced upbringing. The lack of even one parent – for any reason – work timings, divorce or death – has an extremely adverse impact on its upbringing. Adolf Hitler is a prime example of a thoroughly debased child that sprung from a one-parent family.

Parents are as bows that send forth their children as arrows into society. Give your children direction, momentum, and most importantly – meaning. Most people today have the means to live, but no meaning to live for! Meaning gives life purpose and a sense of moral duty. It creates better human beings.

There is only one beautiful child in this world. And every parent has it! Adjust your busy schedules. Reserve time for your children. If you are the only parent looking over your children, try to spend more time with them. Love them. Feed them. Teach them. And try to give them a spiritual outlook on life. If you don't, who will?

CHOOSING THE RIGHT SPOUSE

One of the toughest questions to be faced by parents from their children is "Why can't I marry a person of another caste or religion?"

From the very outset, we all need to realize that nothing in this universe is perfect and therefore there is also no such thing as the 'perfect marriage' either. The rise in divorce rates in every assortment of marriage throughout all sectors of society bears clear testimony to this. But let me share some facts with you.

A very bright and intelligent Indian youth once asked me why in Indian tradition a person should get married to a spouse of their parent's choosing rather than their own.

"Are you a good child?" I asked.

"Yes," he said, a little surprised by the question.

"What do you think of your father and grandfather?"

"They're both great!" he replied.

"And your mother and grandmother?"

"They're both great, too!"

"Did you realize that all of you are the products of arranged marriages?"

The boy was stunned. "I never thought of it that way before," he said appreciatively.

Please don't get me wrong. The final decision concerning whom a sibling should marry should be a family decision rather than an independent one by the children. "If parents oppose a decision made by a child," explains H.H. Pramukh Swami Maharaj, "The children should seek to convince them with patience and should only proceed with the marriage after having first procured their blessings."

Children need to realize that choosing a spouse is probably the biggest and most important decision they will make in their lifetime. And the repercussions of that decision will be felt thereafter in every second and in every area of their lives – their job careers, families, social circles, health and later, their children. If the right decision is made, the couple will live together joyously as an inseparable unit for the rest of their lives – though they may have some differences of opinion on occasions. If the decision is badly flawed however, married life will probably emerge as hell for them and their relatives. And those who will suffer most will be their offspring. The agony of seeing their parents fighting each other is heartbreaking for these innocent children. Even when such couples take care to fight out of sight of their children or to speak in another language, children instinctively pick up the vibrations and know something is amiss. And when the marriage is finally terminated and the parents begin fighting over possession of the children – who ultimately end up living in one-parent families or with a stepparent – the scars in their tender hearts become permanent: they never fully recover. And frighteningly, it has been discovered that these children from one-parent families commit nearly sixty percent of all delinquent crimes! This is why it is so crucial that the best attempt to make the best decision be made. For this, the twenty years experience of parents is invaluable. Children very often search merely for good looks in a spouse or something almost as superficial such as material wealth and luxury. They often forget that appearances are only skin-deep; that beautiful people are not always beautiful on the inside and that plain or plump people are often gorgeous on the inside. This truth, however, is usually realized by them only after the marriage – when it's too late. The consequences are devastating: psychiatrists have rated divorce as the second most traumatic experience of a person's life, after the death of a loved one.

My advice: when a prospective spouse has been pinpointed by either the son, daughter or their parents, the whole family should sit together with a large piece of paper and make two columns: one headed "advantages" and the other "disadvantages". Then they should begin to pen down honestly the specific long-term and short-term advantages and disadvantages of marrying that person in relation to their family, careers, health and future children. Writing these things down on paper will make the actual state of affairs much clearer to everyone and will help the family make a wiser, more practical decision.

A man was sitting in a bus. An observant passenger next to him commented, "You're wearing your wedding ring on the wrong finger." "I know," replied the man gloomily. "I married the wrong woman." That applies both ways. There is much truth in the maxim "Look before you leap!"

PARENT-TEENAGER RELATIONSHIP: PROBLEMS AND SOLUTIONS

It's amazing isn't it? An offspring so genetically similar to its parents can be so different, behaviourally. A major reason is that we are not simply the sum of our genes but also the outcome of our interaction with the world around us. The world has come a long way since the birth of many parents today, who were programmed in an older, less technical environment. Computer technology is advancing so fast that *Computer World* magazine states, "If the auto industry had done what the computer industry has done in the last 30 years, a Rolls Royce would cost $2.30 cents and get 2 million miles to the gallon." So it's not surprising that today's cyberkids find it difficult – if not impossible – to relate to mom and dad and what they say about the "olden days". And vice-versa.

What is the remedy? One thing is categorical: the clock cannot be turned back. In fact, it appears to be racing forward at an ever-increasing pace. Change is necessary for progress. We enjoy air travel, send satellites into orbit, watch telecasts from across the globe, eat fresh fruits from countries thousands of miles away and have cured diseases considered fatal just a few decades ago. We avail of surgery bordering on the miraculous with the use of fiber optics, micro lasers and micro robots. All this has become possible only because our forefathers were prepared to part with the past and change their living patterns drastically from seasonal and manual agricultural labor to round-the-clock machine operation at factories in modern cities. Today, as a result, a single man and his machine or computer can do the job of a thousand people of yore. Who knows what wonders the future holds for our great grandchildren and great, great grandchildren! To bring an end to technological progress would be to deprive them of the relative benefits they would have over our generation just as we have had over the last. We need to find another more practical solution to closing the generation gap and cultivating more affectionate and understanding relationships between parents and siblings. Here are some tips:

Parents

1. Don't compare your child with their other siblings or friends.
2. Don't favour one child over another.
3. Allow them to do house chores at their own convenience (within a few hours).
4. Eradicate personal hypocrisy in the form of double standards. Practice what you preach.
5. Avoid bigotry. If you can't answer their questions, admit it quickly. Then go and find someone who can shed some light on the matter.
6. Don't be too proud to apologize for a mistake or misunderstanding.
7. Do not denigrate their friends.

Children

1. Thank your parents sincerely for the many sacrifices in their personal career, social life and health they must have made in the past and are continuing to make for your benefit without informing you.
2. Even when they are clearly wrong, let them save face. Remember, they are your parents.
3. Don't fight with your brothers or sisters. It hurts your parents tremendously.
4. Study hard. A good education is more important today than has been at any point in history.

5. Keep your room neat and tidy. During vacation periods offer to do all the housework, etc. for mum and let her take the day off: you will realize how hard your parents work.
6. Remember their birthdays and anniversaries.

Above all, don't forget to tell each other "I love you" as often as possible. Being embarrassed or taking it for granted won't do in today's day and age. You have to say it! You must communicate your feelings and emotions openly. And remember there's a time and place for everything - even a thorough argument can be very healthy for a relationship if conducted without sharpness or bitterness.

Last but not least, learn to forgive and forget. A youth once said to a friend, "Whenever I make a mistake, my mum gets historical." "Hysterical, you mean,' corrected the friend. "No. Historical. She goes on to remind me of the day, date and time of every mistake I've made in my life!"

To err is human. To forgive and forget is divine.

FRIENDSHIP...

NEVER MAKE ENEMIES; STRIVE TO MAKE FRIENDS

The world is full of warring brothers, sisters, spouses, communities and nations. The meanings of words such as 'brother' or 'spouse' have become blurred, now referring to a merely technical connection with each other in terms of their DNA or a legal contract rather than the deeper relationships of love, companionship and friendship, as they did previously. The cause of the warring? Old rivalries, old grudges, misunderstandings and conflicts of value systems. The last goes to the root of it all. It is not, as many would like to believe, that most people are inherently deceptive, scheming or selfish. What is intrinsic to people is their value systems – the priorities and hierarchical structures of things they value most in their lives – it may be money, power, adventure, security, health, career, studies, fame, the opposite sex, friends, family or something as simple as food, sports, dancing, partying and sometimes something very much deeper, such as philanthropy, social work or God. Any one of these can take precedence over all the others if it is at the top of his or her value system. And we cannot force someone to renounce his or her values under duress or even through logically justifying our values to be better than theirs. Value systems lie on a deeper level than intellectual systems. For example, in Louisiana, USA, a train crashed over a bridge and fell into the river below. The carriages began to sink rapidly as water flooded into them. Rescue teams arrived shortly, but there was little time to spare. Water had already reached chin level in the compartments. One young couple was trapped with their young cerebral palsy afflicted child. Rescuers reached into the compartment to pull the couple out. Instead, they handed over their baby and perished as their compartment submerged moments later. An act of heroism or foolishness? Both views can be argued vehemently. But arguing changes nothing. For that particular couple, there existed no other option. Saving the baby first was the only thing to do.

Understanding that other people don't always have the same value systems we do, is the first and most crucial step towards creating friendship or resolving strife. It makes it easier for us to let go more often. Too many discussions on trivial matters such as the distance from Mumbai to Delhi end up in argument and bitter exchanges! Learn to laugh and change the topic or just agree or keep quiet. Talk about subjects which interest others, not yourself, even if those subjects are truly boring. Remember, they mean a lot in the value system of the other person. Ask them how they got involved in the subject and about their experiences and opinions. The more people you show interest in, the more friends you'll have. But remember, do not assume that friends are primarily for helping you. That may be disastrous. That thought represents *your* value system. Theirs may just be "friends are for chatting and listening to".

In serious matters, however, all individuals should enter a mutual, written agreement in the company of witnesses from both sides: even with dealings with one's father, brother, wife, son or best friend. Remember, they may not all share the same value system as you – for example – "trust" or "gentlemanship". Or their value systems might easily change in the future. For instance, when young, many people subscribe to the value "all for one and one for all." Later, after many thankless experiences they furiously switch over to "every man for himself." So, if a person refuses to enter into such a written agreement with you, make some excuse and just call off the plan. Even if it sours relations a little, it won't sour them as much as it will years later when people begin to say "I didn't promise any such thing" or "You told me you were going to do this and that." Another important reason for such legal dealings even with those close to us is so that the agreement cannot be contested by other people in the event of the signatory passing away or becoming mentally impaired due to illness, accident or old age, etc.

The master formula is: to get a friend, be a friend. But please choose your friends carefully. Their value system will determine their destiny. Associating with them may determine yours, too.

DOES ANYONE CARE?

Are people really so callous as to just walk past when right before their eyes a woman is being burned to death by an assailant? Are people really so insensitive that scenes of suffering and pain no longer induce feelings of sadness and anguish? Have the people of India and its great states like Maharashtra – the land of the intrepid Shivaji – now become deserters and cowards? Shame on those who just strolled away as Mrs. Vidya Prabhudesai was being doused with kerosene and screaming for help. Not only one person was responsible for the death of this innocent woman. Every person in the vicinity who failed to act have automatically become accomplices to the murderer in the successful accomplishment of his horrible goal.

One problem is that most people are just too busy trying to survive themselves and therefore just don't have other people as a priority on their agenda – even if it means the death of that other person! They already have enough problems of their own and cannot shoulder those of others too. Another reason why people behave so indifferently seems to be because they feel that amongst all the thousands of people who surround them someone will probably come and take care of the situation if they don't. I once read a very telling story posted on the notice board of an office building about four people named Everybody, Somebody, Anybody and Nobody. It goes like this: "There was an important job to be done and Everybody was sure Somebody would do it. Anybody could have done it, but Nobody did it. Somebody got angry about that, because it was Everybody's job. But Everybody thought Anybody could do it, but Nobody realized that Everybody wouldn't do it. It ended up Everybody blamed Somebody, and Somebody blamed Everybody when Nobody did what Anybody could have." Moral: don't wait for somebody to do something or nobody will do it! You must do it; whatever the other tasks you may previously have set out to do – even if it means throwing oneself into a dangerous situation. This is the morality that makes us human beings.

Even animals have a sense of social duty. Have you not seen the local dog defending or barking at a person who is arguing loudly with a person it knows? Elisabeth Gawain tells of the day she went deep sea diving and found herself suddenly short of oxygen. She began to suffocate, got severe and painful cramp and began to sink. She knew she was about to die a watery death on the ocean bed. Just then, she saw the most beautiful thing in the world. It was the eye of a dolphin which had suddenly arrived by her side upon observing her distress. The dolphin lifted her on its back and transported her safely to the shore! If dolphins can go out of their way to help human beings, why can't we humans help each other when in need? Some argue that the law courts summon them as a witness to the incident and too much of their valuable time is wasted. I ask you how many such burnings are you going to witness in your lifetime? How many car accidents with their victims groaning on the ground are you going to witness in your lifetime? One, two, three? And wouldn't you be grateful if somebody helped you when you were in trouble or spent time in the courts for you? Spending time for somebody in the courts is not too high a price to pay if it will save his or her life. The price of living with the feeling of guilt for not preventing a heinous deed or an avoidable death is much higher. It costs you your humanity.

Bhagwan Swaminarayan once awoke in the middle of the night to the cries of a person in adversity. It was pouring with rain and his house had collapsed. The Lord rushed to the site getting drenched in the rain and placed his divine shoulder beneath the main beam of the house while the grateful man moved his children who were trapped inside to a safe distance.

To live without a thought for those who are in trouble is the path of the senseless brute. Living with compassion and care – not only for one's own family – but also of others, is the path of the truly great.

WHAT FRIENDS ARE FOR!

Intent is far more important than content. A child may buy a gift for its parents from the very same pocket money they had given to him. But because the intent of the child is selfless, it still feels like a gift when they take it into their hands. In contrast, a free gift from an elder would appear as a curse when perceived to have vested interests attached.

The greatest and noblest leaders of society have always been those who have been straight and forthright in their speeches, policies and activities. These leaders were not orators, but people who spoke with simple words. They were not handsome, rich or beautiful. But people listened to them; followed them. Nay, they sacrificed their lives for them. It's not money, fame or power most people really want. Deep inside, what they actually crave is a sheltering friendship. Said Henry Ford, "I have been surrounded not by real friends but people who are interested only in my money. If by giving away all my wealth, I could acquire a single friend, I would do it".

A true friend. One who never deserts you. One who is always there when you need him. One who defends, protects and forgives you even when you have wronged. That is a friend. Oh, it's so wonderful to have such a friend! He or she might be in the form of a parent, fellow sibling, relative, colleague, good book or Guru. But a good friend is someone everyone needs.

These friends tell you the bitter truth, but it's easy for you to swallow because you know their intent is pure. You know they are not using the truth to pull you down or hurt you like others do. You know they are using it to pull you up and heal you, like no one else does. Such friends don't have a political agenda in their lives. Unlike today's leaders who have 'no permanent relationships, but only permanent interests', true friends have eternal, unflinching plans for you. Said Bhagwan Swaminarayan to his devotees, "You have come to Me. Therefore I shall liberate you of even the tiniest of flaws. This is My deepest pledge to you." True friends push us towards perfection.

Friends are committed, determined. They put you before themselves. They love you as themselves! They appreciate you more than the whole world put together. They know you through to your bones. They understand every beat of your heart and every frequency of the thought-waves in your brain. They comprehend the agonies of your soul and the ecstasy of your dreams. Yet, they manage to handle them all; controlling your tantrums, calming your nerves and cradling your soul. Isn't this what most people want? Someone to soothe them and assure them everything will be all right in the end?

But such friends are so rare! And only true spiritual mentors live on forever. Parents, spouse and friends pass away. Fellow siblings pursue careers in far off lands. A feeling of loneliness and defencelessness descends on people – however rich or powerful they may be – when they begin to lose their nearest and dearest. But this is life's trademark. In fact, it's life's debacle. Said Chilean writer Isabelle Allende in her beautiful book, *Paula,* which she dedicated to her daughter Paula upon her untimely death, "The loss of my daughter taught me what life is all about. It's about losing everything."

We cannot prevent our closest ones from leaving us alone in this harsh, wild world. But their intent in leaving us is pure too: they are nudging us to take their place as selfless friend and guardian of someone else! We must follow their footsteps and tread their path. As they were unto us, we must be unto others. But remember, even if you can't be as helpful as the friend who helped and guided you, you can still bear his essential qualities: a pure and pristine intention. Most of us will never do great things, but we can all do small things in this great, selfless way!

THE EFFECTS OF FRIENDS AND COMPANY

"Tell me thy company and I'll tell thee what thou art," announced Cervantes, the celebrated Spanish playwright.

How true! Adolf Hitler was a "sunny, well turned-out, companionable and intelligent child," reveal historians. But during his youth he associated with a fascist named Dr. Potsch who converted him into an eternal and inimitable monster who through World War 2 caused the death of 55 million people! The lovely and cuddly Hitler became a fascist fiend through association with negative elements. Conversely, at Sing Sing Prison in the U.S. in the 1930s, prisoners who had been convicted of the most violent and gruesome murders and sentenced to life imprisonment became timid and caring human beings under the loving attention of Catherine Lawes – the philanthropic wife of the prison warden. Upon her sad and untimely death in an accident, these prisoners were reduced to tears and were allowed to visit her body to pay their last respects at her home some two kilometres away. The lady had transformed their hearts so deeply that the prison authorities allowed them to leave the prison without any guards, surveillance or handcuffs and merely instructed them to be back by 5 p.m.! And by 5 p.m. sharp, every single one of them had returned to the prison to complete their life sentences! This is the power – positive and negative – that different types of company can exert on people and their behaviour. An innocent child can be turned into a Hitler and a Hitler can be turned into an innocent child.

Human beings possess an innate capacity to form loving relationships with parents, relatives and friends. They also have the brilliant potential to build space shuttles and soar into orbit

around the Earth, to achieve doctorates in several subjects, to write and speak eloquently in several languages, to play several musical instruments and also to contemplate the meaning of life and delve within to seek the divine self and the transcendent God. All of the above can be achieved in a single lifetime if one has the right environment and associates from whom to learn the required skills. But without such wholesome company man cannot grow much beyond the animal. In the 1800s, scientists discovered a wild boy living in a French jungle. He didn't stand upright and walked on all fours like a wolf. He sniffed at food with his nose before he ate it and could make no sounds other than snorts and grunts. The boy was captured and taken back to the city where he was washed, cleaned, his hair cut and his body clothed. Psychologists and social workers tried to rehabilitate him and teach him to walk, talk and count. But, all efforts were in vain. He failed to respond to them intellectually, socially and emotionally - and simply sat sitting crouched in a corner. This is an example of how retarded the development of a person can be if he or she does not receive correct nurturing, not only during childhood but also during teen years.

An MBBS student once came to me in a gloomy and dispirited mood. "I can't bring myself to study anymore," he said. "It is not worth the effort. My friends live so easily and they all drive Maruti cars." "What do they do for a living?" I asked. The answer was revealing, "They run *pau bhaji* stalls," he replied. "Try to make friends with youths who are more like yourself," I advised him. An MBBS student cannot remain motivated if he is going to hang around with friends who run *pau bhaji* stalls. He or she has to associate with people who are pursuing brilliant careers themselves.

In all your walks of life - personal, social and spiritual - try to befriend people who are positive about themselves, who think big, see long-term and are aware of the larger picture - material and spiritual. They are the ones who will inspire and motivate you. These are the associates who will bring the best out of you: the angel and the marvel.

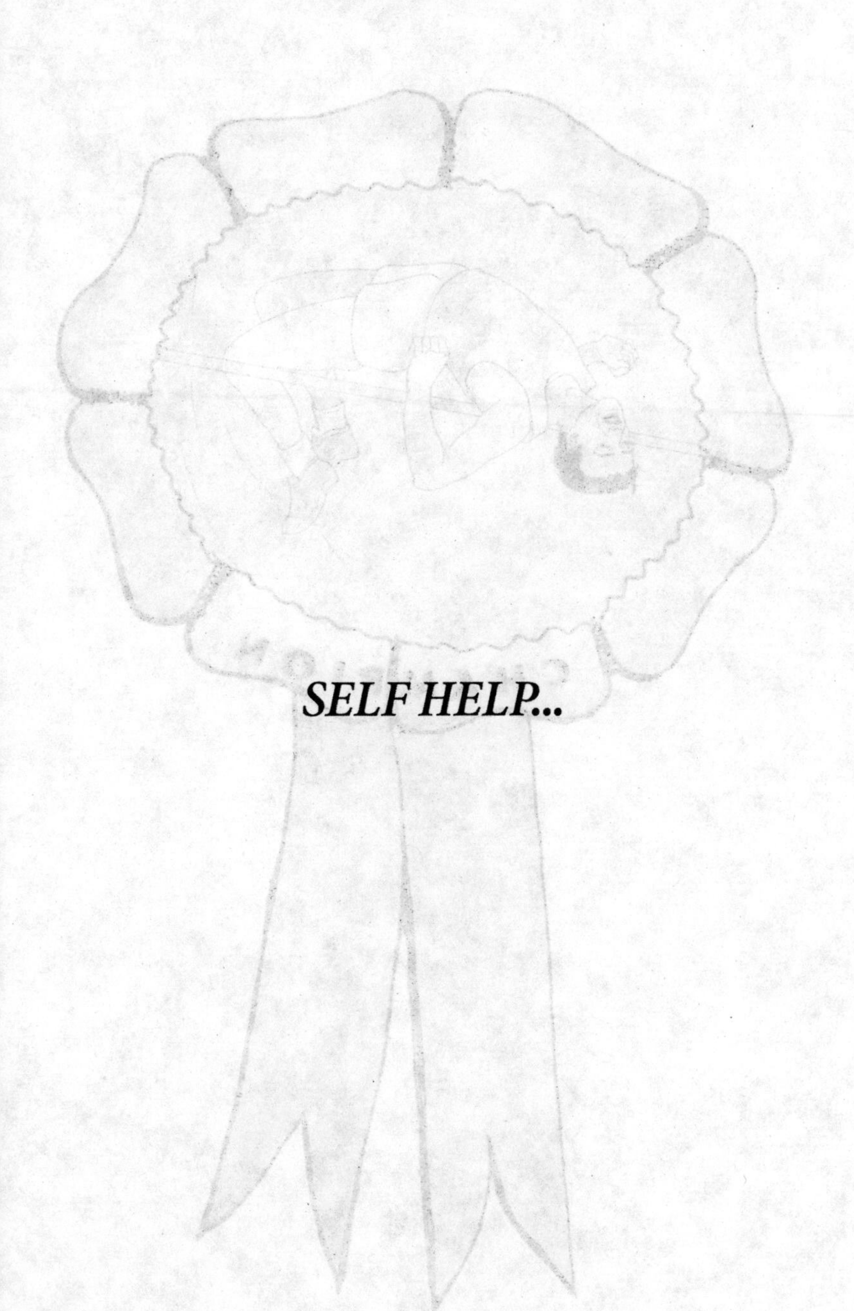

SELF HELP...

CHAMPION

ABOUT WINNING AND LOSING

A young and ambitious boy decided to become the greatest batsman in the world. Playing alone, he tossed the ball in the air and swung with his bat. He missed. He tried again. He missed. He tried a third time. He missed again. "Oh well," he said cheerfully. "Because my bowling is so good, maybe I'll become the best bowler in the world!"

What's the difference between winning and losing? That depends on what type of software you have loaded into your brain. A software package which responds with the statement, "An illegal command has been operated. The system is closing down," is not the best of packages. One which says "Attempting Recovery Now" is far better. A lot of people need to install this new software in their brains - urgently. From this new package they will quickly realize a number of eternal facts about winning and losing.

One idea about winning which is simply not true, is that winning means excelling above everyone else in the world. It doesn't. Winning really means becoming better than you were yesterday! It means improving and breaking your own records, not somebody else's. Even a person who achieves a place in the Guinness Book of Records but could have done better still had he or she tried harder, cannot be termed a true success. This is not to say that achieving a place in the Guinness Book of Records is worthless: only that it should not become a goal, an ambition. If it happens as a sort of side effect, so be it. Success consists of being, becoming and achieving the best you can whether or not your achievement is noted by a world record book. A student that could have achieved 98% in his or her examinations is not a genuine success if he or she actually achieves "only" 95% due to laziness. But a weak student who achieves only 40% but really tried his or her level best is a true success. This goes for all vocations in life. It even includes areas such as parenthood and other family or social relationships. Trying one's hardest to make things as best as they can possibly be in the circumstances is what it means to be a winner.

Circumstances and environment play a major role in the "success" of a person. This cannot be denied. No man or woman is an island. Everyone depends on other people and a conducive environment to make their dreams come true. Einstein discovered the Theory of Relativity partly because he was born during a period in Germany when science was at its heights and all the groundwork in mathematics which he needed such as Riemannian Geometry and Lorentz Coordinate Transformation formulae had already been laid. Einstein was left only to arrange the pieces. From this perspective, Isaac Newton was much greater. He had to create much of the mathematics - such as calculus - all by himself to formulate his scientific theories. And Galileo was greater still for he had even less mathematics than Newton at his disposal and lived at a time when most people around him believed the Earth was flat and at the centre of the universe! Amitabh Bachan would be just another Indian doctor or engineer practicing in the U.S. had he been born there. Bill Gates would be nothing, had he been born in the Congo. Prince Harry and William would be ordinary teenagers rather than future kings, had they been born in another family. One billion people in India would be more successful than those living in the western world or Japan today - had their political leaders not failed to supply them an education after Independence, in accordance with their promise.

Circumstances must be taken into account if we are to make a fair and non-biased appraisal of a person's or nation's achievements. Assessing them in isolation of their environment creates serious distortion. And it is this distortion which creates false feelings of inferiority; thoughts of being a loser, a failure. Millions of people are afflicted by such unfounded, illogical notions and assumptions and they continue to needlessly whip themselves over it day in and day out, creating their own distress and depression.

Discard these unrealistic notions and decide to be happy about your achievements. Be the best you can possibly be in the circumstances God has put you in and you can legitimately consider yourself one of the most successful people in the world.

BEING GOOD IN A CROOKED WORLD

A medieval scholar once commented, "I'm not sure whether the world is round or flat. But I certainly know it's crooked!" Out of fifty four countries recently appraised by international businessmen, India was rated the ninth most corrupt country in the world with Pakistan coming in second and Nigeria first. (New Zealand was the least corrupt). Corruption has become the name of the game. If you want to get people to do things, the formula is: first try to convince'em – if that doesn't work confuse'em – and if that doesn't work – corrupt'em. The chairmanship, the presidency and the world title go to the highest bidder. In this world where money is everything, Mr. Average stands little chance unless he follows suit – "If you can't beat them, join them," they say.

But most people aren't corrupt. And even if they are, most of them don't enjoy being corrupt. Who likes to give their money away as a bribe for something that is legally entitled to them? But, unless a paperweight is submitted with most requests, work procedures are stalled and the requester unable to continue normally with his or her life and career.

One of the problems is India's casual, easy-go-style. Like bargaining with a storekeeper at a market for a kilogram of tomatoes or an imitation article, corruption has become a way of life; a given. As such, people from gatemen to statesmen have internalized this habit without fully realizing its seriousness and long term consequences. To a certain extent, they have convinced themselves that it may not really be such a bad thing after all – just a gratuitous tip for service – a token of their probity and chivalry.

Probity? Chivalry? Connivance and cowardly surrender is more like it! If people have extra money to splash out on bribes, they should give it to charity. Corruption needs to be obliterated – root and branch. If government or private enterprises genuinely require more money, they should hike their prices and acquire their finances over the table, not from under it. Honesty is a far more valuable asset to society and vastly more preferable than acquiring fat profits from selling adulterated diesel, diluted milk, substandard fruits and grain and inferior construction material for roads and buildings. The presence of corruption in the world is a direct consequence of good people sitting on their hands when they should be standing on their feet. It is literally the price of an undemanding, passive and totally fatalistic public. In many countries abroad, consumers refuse to buy dubious or even slightly defective products.

The power to change things lies with the people, more importantly, with ordinary people. Heroes are ordinary men and women who do extraordinary things. Rosa Parks has become immortal for refusing to vacate her seat for a white man on an American bus at Montgomery – sparking the black freedom movement by Martin Luther King Jr.. Mahatma Gandhi – voted Man of the Century by *The Times Of India* and Man of the Century Runner up by *Time International* magazine – refused to be a foreigner in his own country and lead the Salt Marches that ultimately uprooted the British Empire. Indira Gandhi commanded the Indian army to remove the women of Gujarat who were patrolling election booths – and to use tear gas or even live rounds if necessary – but the army refused to shoot at its own people. Precisely the same thing occurred in Russia, leading to the fall of communism. Young children, too, can become heroes like the eight-year old Jinabhai (Yogiji Maharaj) who took the courageous step of reporting to the headmaster the violent conduct of his teacher against another pupil, when all the other children were afraid to speak out from fear of becoming victims of the teacher themselves.

Everyone can do their little bit once in a while to make our country, and ultimately the world much straighter and the path along which we must all tread smoother, faster and richer.

FOLLOW YOUR OWN PATH

What a complex world we live in! More than 170 nations, a thousand cultures, thousands of languages and dialects, hundreds of religions, a thousand philosophies - all mixed together with a thousand superstitions, stereotypes and biases!

Untangling this carnival of chaos by attempting to educate and enlighten each and every individual in the world is entirely unachievable within a time frame of a few years, though it could certainly be achieved within ten decades if all the world's leaders would become enlightened first, unite and then work for the common good of our planet. Sometimes educating even the loved ones around us - such as parents or spouse, brothers, sisters and friends - seems an almost impossible task, too - let alone trying to convince the rest of the world. The reason is because every person on this earth has had a unique upbringing – familial, physical, educational, social and spiritual. Even genetically identical twins will have slightly different character and personality traits. One of the oldest Hindu scriptures in the world, the Rig Veda, expounded on the very same directive explaining that "Two friends having identical eyes and ears will still be dissimilar in their mental inclinations." No two people in this world are exactly alike. Everyone is an individual. Some people like spicy foods, others don't. Some like travelling, some don't. Some like chatting, some prefer quiet and reflection. Some like Rock, others prefer classical... The list of preferences and abhorrences is infinite!

What should be done? Take your own route. Do your own thing. Be yourself. Consult others, but leave the final decision to yourself. You must decide what is right and what is wrong – what is bad, good, better and best. And do not make the mistake of trying to please everybody – today, that is almost impossible. Whatever you do, there will always be someone somewhere in the world who will criticize you or your actions. Similarly, there will always be someone somewhere who will agree with your decision and will praise you profusely for it! So discard from your mind the tensions and anxieties that result from people's comments: keep faith in yourself. Strive hard and push ahead.

Once, Shivji and Parvati were journeying with their bull. Shivji sat on the bull while Parvati walked beside. At the first village they passed, people criticized them, "Look. The man sits upon the bull while he makes the woman walk beside." Shivji got down and sat Parvati on the bull. At the next village, people criticized them, "Look. The woman sits upon the bull and makes her husband walk beside." Shivji climbed up and sat along with Parvati on the bull. At the third village the people criticized them, "Look. The man and woman have no mercy on the bull and sit upon it with all their weight." Both got down and walked alongside the bull. At the fourth village people criticized, "Look at these two fools! What is the use of taking along the bull if neither is going to sit on it?"

Of course, we are not advocating that you become reckless or disobedient to elders. Sometimes you certainly do have to put your pride aside and seriously consider what parents, relatives, spiritual mentors and our holy scriptures are telling you. Remember, in times of difficulty it is only these people who will be there to support you. So think very carefully before taking any major step. And remember the process of thinking or planning should not become an excuse for procrastination, nor should fear of failure paralyze your decision-making or your efforts. You have to be courageous. If something doesn't work out as you expected, find out why and take good measure to ensure you don't make the same mistake again. You should also use such incidents to teach you alternative and superior methods of doing things in future. This way, you will make personal, social and spiritual progress in great leaps and bounds.

A famous judge was once asked by a reporter the secret behind his success. "Good decisions," the judge replied. "But what is the secret behind your making good decisions?" "Experience," said the judge. "Yes," continued the reporter, a little exasperated. "But what is the secret behind your experience?" "Bad decisions," replied the judge.

Learn from your mistakes. Walk the path prescribed by our holy scriptures, sadhus and mentors.

LIFE: A UNIQUE OPPORTUNITY

"To be, or not to be?" is the classic question by the famous Shakespearean character, Hamlet, as he soliloquized his personal option of suicide upon the untimely death of his father. The satirical French playwright and thinker, Voltaire, has given the answer to anyone else contemplating the same option. "People who commit suicide," he wrote in one of his short and stimulating essays "would have wished to live if only they had waited a few weeks."

Every year in the US alone, nearly 200,000 people attempt suicide that's nearly one percent of the population! More than 30,000 of those attempts lead to fatalities. The "Land of Golden Opportunity" is also the land of frustrated careers, relationships and desires. In the distorted perspective these despairing and pessimistic individuals unwittingly create in their minds, they overlook the biggest opportunity of all; the choice to live, to continue, to strive, to get up and try again or to experiment with something new, something different from what they were previously doing. Life, even when seemingly bereft of anything else, in reality lies silently with the dormant seeds of all opportunities. Life, not death is the answer to our problems. Suicide itself is the greatest of failures, far exceeding the failure of any marriage or career! It is the greatest self defeating action one can take. Fleeing from life is as irrational as a sick person fleeing from his doctor or the hospital! Marilyn Monroe, Elvis Presley,... were all people who had the greatest of opportunities: more than their fair share compared to ordinary folk. Yet, they overlooked this and took their own lives even though they still had decades of fertile time ahead of them. They threw away their entire lives to escape a few moments of distress.

The fulfilment of personal, materialistic and often childish ambitions are not life's biggest opportunities by any means. What people really need is less of ambition and more of mission. A person who has no cause to die for usually has no purpose to live for either. He or she is neither alive nor dead. People who have missions such as family, helping the needy, welfare campaigns, disaster-relief work, civilian rights, freedom, humanitarianism and self-realisation recognize the dignity and glory of human life. They know life is a unique opportunity for all rich and poor and that all, including themselves, should enjoy life to its fullest length as well as depth. Whatever the quality of your existence, remember it is still a human existence and therefore priceless. Gold is gold whatever shape it is in! Life is life whatever way it shapes out. It cannot be thrown away, trashed out.

Survivors of terminal or life threatening diseases such as cancer often comment that the disruption and often complete termination of their careers brought about by the illness actually awakened them to simpler but more valuable things in life, things we are often too engrossed in our mechanical routines to notice or try: watching the sun rise and set, witnessing the beauty of the moon, paddling barefooted in a stream, chomping into a juicy melon, chatting into the night, laughing, blowing dandelions and relishing the fragrance of roses or freshly cut grass, listening to the sound of children laughing or watching them play on the swings and roundabouts at a park, understanding the glory and greatness of God, the list is endless!

These people actually thank God for wakening them to the simpler, truer rewards of life and also to its longer term spiritual dimension. Like a child knows little more than the toys it plays with, oblivious of the wider context of its own past and future, those who commit suicide do so oblivious to the more important, spiritual aspects of life. This is why most religions condemn suicide even in the most extenuating circumstances when a person has little or no reason to live. Bhagwan Swaminarayan states it quite categorically: the great and only fortune of human life is the opportunity to offer our devotions to God. Echoed Mary Brindell when struck with cancer, "It was then I really realized how simple God's plan is. Yet how complicated we humans have made his Earth. Nothing really matters but those truths and principles which already exist deep in our hearts. You only need to look deep enough to find them." Hamlet! Live and let live.

STOP WORRYING!

"What if...?" "How will...?" "Who will...?" "Where will...?" "When will...?" These are the five insidious and entrapping questions that lead people to fret and worry. It would be wonderful if worrying was equivalent to thinking. Then all the problems of the world would be over. But worrying isn't the same as thinking - in fact, it hinders it - rendering its victims paraplegic patients of the negative emotions it creates - fear, anxiety, tension and stress. These emotional afflictions turn against them too, depleting their energy and weakening their immune systems. They literally become sick from worrying - suffering from poor and fragile health not so much because of what they eat, but because of what is eating them!

Worry usually occurs when we find ourselves faced with an outcome we feel is beyond the scope of our control - an outcome we have predicted will be wholly damaging and detrimental to us. But we can never be really certain of this. Some good might come out of it as well. So what sense lies in despairing and agonizing oneself over something that may actually turn out well, or if it does not, its long-term repercussions do? An example: a king accidentally lost his little finger in an accident. His close friend and minister, however, exclaimed that it was a fine thing that had happened! The king therefore expelled him upon which the minister concluded even his expulsion was also a good thing! This puzzled the king. Some time later, the king got lost during a hunting expedition in a jungle and was captured by cannibals. They were about to fry him in a pot when they suddenly noticed he had a finger missing. An incomplete human being was unacceptable to the gods, so they released him. The king realized

that losing his finger earlier, had saved his life later. "But tell me," he asked after returning to the palace and reinstating his minister, "what good came out of me expelling you? You temporarily lost your wages and prestige." "If you had not expelled me," said the minister, "I would probably have accompanied you in the jungle and both of us would have been caught by the cannibals. You would be back here safely today, but because my body is whole, I wouldn't!"

The chain of cause and effect is extremely subtle. The slightest, invisible variation in an event could well lead to dramatic consequences in the future. Therefore it is almost impossible to predict what will happen in the long-term, and whether it will be good or bad because we cannot know all the variables precisely. Neither do we know how the fortunes and misfortunes of other people may forward or reverse ours – or for that matter, too, how our fortunes or misfortunes may affect those of others. It is a very small world and we are buffeting each other all the time.

Therefore look at life as a long chain of surprises and new revelations. This is what life truly is. So live it with a strong and robust spirit of sportsmanship. The goal of life is not to achieve some mythical point of perfect materialism. No such apex exists. The goal of life is simply to work hard at becoming better than you were yesterday. One has not to shatter the records of others, but only one's own. That is what it means to be a winner and this is all it should take to make you happy and free of unnecessary worry.

The crucial point to remember always is that in life, there are no wars to be won – only battles to be fought – personal, physical, social, psychological and spiritual. And no-one fights alone, too. God is the eternal comrade, the invisible companion, the universal friend. But be very sure – God will fight with you but not for you! His Divine Holiness Pramukh Swami Maharaj was once approached three times by a person asking for blessings that his new business runs well. His Holiness sweetly admonished him, "Please understand," he said. "The blessings were not upon you, but upon your efforts. Now you have to start working." These golden words weld together the interface between spiritual thinking and practical living. A seed cannot sprout without rains. Nor can rains make green a land bereft of seeds. God will certainly build for you a beautiful castle – if not in the sky then in your heart – but you must first go and put the foundation beneath it.

STRESS MANAGEMENT

Stress management? Easy!! Down a beer, smoke a cigarette, drink some tea or coffee, watch television right? No! A thousand times, no! Of course there are more legitimate treatments which thousands of people are trying such as massage, aromatherapy, acupuncture, exercise, music and Prozac. But easy come, easy go. What needs to be treated is the cause, not the symptoms. Some causes are quite trivial, such as poor time-management leading to breached deadlines and a warning from the boss. A second cause is a failure to decide priorities, leading to the completion of hundreds of "unimportant" tasks say, at the office and the neglect of one very important responsibility say, a child's upbringing or a marital tension.

Putting aside these two amendable areas, let us focus on circumstances which really are beyond our human capacity to control yet we feel compelled to, nevertheless. Doctors have discovered it is this feeling of compulsion combined with helplessness that leads to the psycho-physiological symptoms of stress: anxiety, insomnia, lethargy, irritability, depression, weakened immune system, high BP, cardiovascular problems and atherosclerosis.

Stress isn't anyone's delicacy. So why do people whip themselves to work so hard, even though matters are totally beyond their scope of control? The fact is, Dr Dean Ornish explains in his best selling book *Reversing Heart Disease Without Medicine or Surgery* that deep within the psyche even the rich and famous people feel inadequate and lacking in some personal area and consequentially isolated even though they may actually be in the midst and approval of hundreds or even thousands of people!

Because of these feelings of loss or lack they feel, "If only I had more money, or more power, more parental approval, more brains, education, talent, more friends, athletic ability, better looks or a thinner waist then people would acknowledge me, appreciate me, love me and then I'd be happy and fulfiled."

Rot. The bottom line is, feelings of self esteem or self worth can only come from within, from your own soul and never from anybody else's sanction. There exists no worldly basis for establishing a true foundation for one's self esteem: ideas about worth and value change in different circumstances and are truly subjective. So don't worry about becoming or not becoming something. In principle and in practice, you just have to be. And the good news is, what you are already your spiritual self is greater than any human power or material object in this universe! Whether or not somebody else can appreciate this fundamental truth or not is immaterial. When you appreciate it and live by it – it is enough. Investing one's self esteem in material things and enjoyments is as irrational as pouring one's money into a collapsing bank. For such investors, losing doesn't mean just losing, it means being a loser. Failing doesn't mean just failing, it means being a failure. The sad truth is 99 percent of people invest this way. One individual while talking to another wonders whether the other thinks he or she is a success, attractive or intelligent while the other is thinking precisely the same thing about him or her!

Nearly everyone wants to be soothed by the appreciation of others. Said tennis superstar Boris Becker in an interview with *World Tennis* magazine, "I wanted to find love and friendship through sports. That's where I found my self approval... I very frequently think about the meaning of life because I live through so many extreme moments. I cannot do more than win Wimbledon... I thought more than once that it wouldn't be so bad if I died at that moment." The Royal Bank of Canada devoted one of its monthly letters to this almost ubiquitous problem with the title *Let's Slow Down*. "We are victims of mounting tension," it wrote. "We have difficulty relaxing: we are not living fully."

Solution: try to do things slowly, without pressure. Don't keep "going for the kill" with deadlines in every matter. Once you realize where the pain in your life is coming from, it becomes easier to discard it. "One needs awareness," says Pramukh Swami Maharaj. And, he adds, "Whatever you think may happen, never keep tension. It merely makes you irritable and impatient. Remain peaceful. God is the all doer, not us. Understanding this ultimate truth brings peace to the soul." We must stop trying to play God and take back our position as clerks. Stress is only a symptom of trying to become something one isn't. Stress management: you may call it managing one's ego.

THE FRUITS OF FEARLESSNESS

Fear: the dark, cold prison of the misguided mind. There are no damp stonewalls, no barred windows, no guards. Yet, the fear-struck mind is probably the most formidable of shackles. Even an escape artist like the legendary Harry Houdini could still be a prisoner of his own psyche.

In some cases, an individual's fear snowballs uncontrollably, resulting in a phobia. These are somewhat illogical and unwarranted fears: the internal giant cowers and quivers before a house mouse, kitten, puppy or even wor – a friendly human being. A jumbo jet was once forced to land only minutes after take-off to allow a screaming and panic-stricken passenger to disembark!

Almost everyone is sometimes paralyzed by fear, though not always so dramatically, in some area of their lives and it behooves them to overcome their fear if they wish to taste the succulent fruits of a life judiciously lived.

In an older year, we may well have sympathized with a person for being chickenhearted. Indeed, he or she had great reason. In the 17th century, petty theft was punishable by death in the courts and professing the Earth was round was heretical in the Church: Galileo nearly paid with his life! But today, in good democracies, fear is unfounded. Yet it persists: the fear of ridicule, looking foolish, looking different, making a mistake or failing. Such fears prevent people from making the leaps that vault them across the terrain they need to conquer. In meetings, they fail to contribute, sitting huddled in a corner, head down, twiddling their thumbs. In class, they slave to work things out in their heads, instead of asking the teacher or a friend. At home, they sit quietly, feigning innocence when all that is required is to say, "I did it. I'm sorry."

Man need fear nothing but fear itself. He who fears fear overcomes it. The odd thing is that fear is not something which originates from our surroundings but from within our own skulls. It's just the way we perceive things. It's the stories we tell ourselves. We create our own fears, get frightened by them and try to make a quick get away! It's a classic case of Catch 22 circular logic, a self-fulfiling prophecy. Each man and woman becomes their own homegrown Nostradamus; each a soothsayer with their own crystal ball; each predicting their own doom. It takes a lot of self-reflection to realize the crystal ball they are peering into is nothing more than their own brain situated directly above their two eyes.

How does one overcome one's fear? Simple. You must do the thing you fear doing. You must walk through the dark passage to prove to yourself no one is there. You must talk to the stranger to realize he is friendly. You must speak up at a meeting to realize your views count. Whatever it is you fear doing – public speaking, making new friends, approaching your boss for a raise, talking to your spouse about a problem or mutual conflict, or saying no to somebody's request – it's best to convince yourself you have nothing to be afraid of simply by doing it. Just do it.

Nothing teaches better than experience. That's what life is all about. Learning. Learning about one's own mind, its illusions, errors and exaggerations.

The result is like bursting through dark clouds into the warm sunlight above and witnessing new horizons one never knew existed.

By far, however, the most effective way to overcome fear is to tap the power of God. With the Lord's strength David could fell Goliath, Arjun could vanquish the Kauravs, Lincoln could defeat the Confederates and Gandhi could oust the British. "He who knows God, overcomes the greatest of fears," says Bhagwan Swaminarayan in his Vanchanamrut sermons. Echoed the celebrated psychoanalyst Carl Jung in his famous book *Modern Man in Search of a Soul,* "Among all my patients in the second half of life; that is to say, over thirty-five years, there has not been one whose problem in the last resort was not that of finding a religious outlook in life."

But don't do anything foolish or immoral. Such actions will certainly have painful consequences – physical, legal, social and spiritual.

THE HIGH THAT DRAGS YOU DOWN

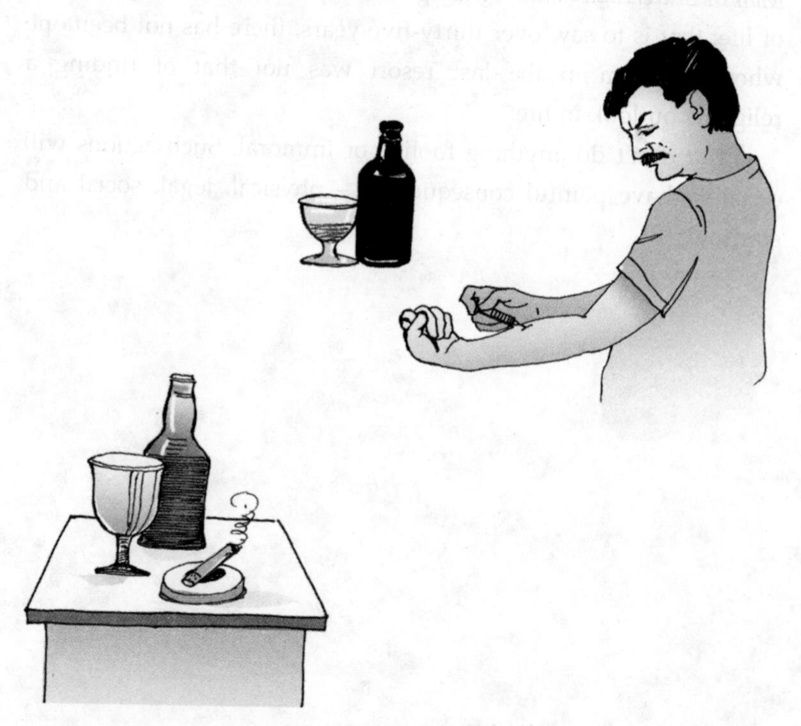

Addiction to drugs – in the form of heroin, brown sugar, cocaine, cigarettes, alcohol, chewing tobacco, glue-sniffing or even downing whole bottles of cough syrup containing codeine – collectively comprise one of the largest causes of human fatalities in the world.

Why are so many people around the globe turning to drugs? The major and root reason – even underlying that of peer pressure and broken families – is because we live as doctors and psychologists declare, in an "Age of Depression". For instance, in Bhuj, it has recently been unearthed that consumption of alcohol and tobacco has soared after the earthquake. Likewise, people all around the world stricken by environmental, social or personal afflictions are desperately trying to find relief through smoking, drinking, swallowing sedatives or injecting drugs. Millions of others resort to compulsive sex, watching television or films, or eating and sleeping. All of these forms of addiction - physiological and psychological - are harmful, but those related to hard drugs such as cocaine or alcohol are even more devastating than environmental disasters like the Bhuj earthquake! This is because addictions usually lead to 1) financial bankruptcy through excessive expenditure and consequent gambling and 2) loss of loved ones - spouse, children, brothers and sisters - through violence and consequent divorce - all at one's own hands!

Can a person permanently kick his or her addiction? Mark Twain once quipped, "Quitting smoking is easy. I've done it hundreds of times."

You may take heart. Bhagwan Swaminarayan promises in His Vachanamrut sermons that overcoming one's addictions is indeed possible! "Any bad habit," assures Bhagwan Swaminarayan, "can be totally annihilated if one cultivates a warrior spirit against it - realizing that the habit is not one's friend, but most malignant enemy." The soul has strength enough to vanquish any internal foe - even if that foe has subdued you for decades. It is a spiritual fact that if you have been subdued, it has been your fault. You allowed it to subdue you. Somewhere deep down in your heart you have viewed it as your friend - something that comforts you and gives you quick, warm relief from your anxiety and depression. And it is this soft corner for your bad habits that ultimately leaves you conquered and crushed. One must truly understand that the object one has befriended is actually an absolute foe. Once you change your perception of your negative activities, your resistance to them will balloon exponentially and you will liberate yourself. Like a captured *jawan* in enemy hands, you will not give in to any amount of physical or psychological torture by the enemy who is bent on slaughtering you, your family, friends and country's citizens!

There will also be other important amendments you will have to make. You will have to renounce your ego and apologize to your family for everything you have done till now. They blame you for it. And they are right. Beg their forgiveness. Ask them for their moral support and love. And as far as possible, give up all company and friends who drink – even if they do so in moderation. A drug addict in Georgia, USA, for example, kicked her habit. Overconfident, she returned to her drug-addicted friends. After five or six visits she was hooked again and was soon behind bars for possession of illicit drugs. Another precaution: never keep extra money in your pocket which might fetch you a quick dose. Make new friends and develop a new attitude towards your tensions and anxieties. Start life afresh.

And beware! Your mind will play cunning games with you. An alcoholic, for instance, once announced at the bar that his will power was so strong he was giving up alcohol forever. The same evening he returned and affirmed, "I have become so mighty I am now stronger than my own will power! Please hand me a double whisky!"

Mind games. That's what kicking the habit is all about.

THE NEED FOR TOLERANCE

"There are two things I will never tolerate," announced the drunkard. "Racial prejudice and Blacks." Intolerance, however, does not refer only to racial prejudice, religious fanaticism and class or gender discrimination. Intolerance also comes in the subtler form of impatience, quick temper or even physical aggression to achieve a goal or acquire an object of one's fancy. The goal might be attempting to get ahead of others in a traffic jam or trying to board a packed train or bus. The object could be anything too – even something as trivial as an item of food, a toy or a newspaper. The result: shoving one's way into a crowded lift at work instead of waiting in the queue; going home and shouting at mum or the wife if dinner is not ready on time and vehemently arguing with a friend or colleague who subscribes to a differing opinion or philosophy to one's own. Intolerant people are unable to endure even the slightest inconvenience – physical or intellectual – caused by another human being.

Whether the other person is at fault or not is another issue. Becoming impatient and yelling one's head off, going into a huff or getting physical are certainly not very good ways of responding to an inconvenience. A better method or technique would be to find out why a person or a situation which causes you inconvenience has arisen in the first place. Ironically, you may find that you yourself are exacerbating or maybe even initiating the succession of events that disturb you. In such circumstances, it would behoove you to help yourself first, so that others can help you better. If you're not to blame anywhere along the line, then going deeper into the problems others face will help you to understand their difficulties, sympathize with them and endure your "ordeals" more graciously. Doing this little extra detective work will also help you to help them find a valid and practical solution to their troubles.

If none of this works despite your good and well-intentioned efforts, one should try to realize that people will be people and that they are what they are because of the type of upbringing they have had. Try to remember that if you were born in identical circumstances with an identical upbringing, you would almost certainly be very similar to the way they are now. Therefore, try to be lenient on others and forgive them. Give more importance to their innocent personality rather than their human faults and ineptness in their actions. Remember, their intentions are not bad, only their management. We also need to remember that we all have our own faults which others have to tolerate, too. They may not be in the same areas that we are usually irritated by, but they are in areas which irritate them! Therefore, be strict and demanding not on the people around you, but on yourself.

Try to be more positive about others. Become completely and thoroughly adaptable and flexible. This will be your strength. For now at least - accept the situation as it is. Don't fight it. Reform it. And the easiest and fastest way to reform a situation is by reforming oneself. To make oneself perfect first is the most simple, but probably least used method to make the world perfect. People seem to have calculated that converting six billion people is easier than converting oneself. Gunatitanand Swami, the foremost disciple of Bhagwan Swaminarayan, used to say, "If everyone used the same forcefulness for making others understand to make themselves understand, there would be no deficiencies left in anyone." Everyone becomes perfect. What an achievement! And those who achieve perfection see what is perfect in others. Imperfections around one are certainly objective facts, but one perceives them only because one is imperfect oneself. Isn't this something we all need to take cognizance of?

Isn't this something which should worry us more? We worry over the deficiencies of our bank account, health, education and career, but we overlook the greater, more deeper and serious deficiencies of our mind and soul. This is the tragedy of the human intellect. The human creature is engrossed only at looking at the perfections and imperfections of the external world, but does not look within to see the perfections and imperfections of the world within.

So let us all give up our misdirected efforts in trying to force others to change. If they are to be changed, the thirst for it has to come from within them. As the proverb goes, "You can take a horse to water, but you can't force it to drink". But maybe it could be inspired to drink if we begin drinking some water first.

WHEN LIFE HURTS, IT TEACHES

For some, the pursuit of happiness is like a blind man in a dark room searching for a black cat that isn't there! Others think happiness is within sight but beyond reach like the proverbial carrot dangling before a donkey's mouth. The majority, however, have the carrot right in their mouths and yet deep down they feel disturbed, frustrated and miserable. This is because their wounds are inside – they are hurting from within. Some time in their past, services were forgotten. Honours were obstructed. Apologies were never offered. Compensation was insufficient. Judgment was unjust. Loyalty was never reciprocated. Love was unacknowledged.

Many feel they must find a way to avoid further pain in their lives. However, a life without pain is impossible. We should not waste time and energy trying to avoid pain. Indeed, we need to accept it as a part and parcel of life and try to learn something from it.

Nothing happens without a purpose. Pain is a clarion call. It is information given to you, that's all. When a person places his hand on a hot stove and scorches his skin, the stove is not punishing him it is merely telling him to quickly move to a safe distance, or else he may come to greater harm. When a person suffers the pain of a kidney stone, the stone is not punishing him, but explaining to him something about his body and diet. In instances of extreme pain – emotional or physical nature is informing us that we are searching for happiness in entirely the wrong direction and something needs to be changed drastically.

We must all go through experiences bitter or sweet. So why not grow through them, as well? Raise yourself to your higher and more powerful self. Try not to go to "pity parties" and wallow in your lower state – self pity, grudges, grievances and bitter memories. Take charge of your life and cherish the lessons you learn. These lessons are your true wealth. The more lessons you have learned, the richer you are! They make you richer than even the richest people in the world who have failed to learn from their past. You will have lived life to the fullest. You will have flown to the heights of life and also touched its depths. You will have enjoyed all its dimensions and all its benedictions. You will have missed nothing. For such persons, even the approach of death which is the worst thing that can happen – is a wonderful lesson! Death becomes the final flowering – the last act, the masterstroke, the crowning glory of a life well lived.

In life, when one door to happiness closes, another even better one opens! You just have to stop staring at the door that has closed and turn your attention somewhere else or even somewhere within yourself. Maybe you've missed something more important. Maybe you've overlooked or forgotten something your mother or father taught you long ago, something you had long concluded yourself.

In New York City, at the Institute of Physical and Medical Rehabilitation, there is a bronze plaque riveted to the wall. The inscription has been copied from the diary of an unknown confederate soldier:

"I asked God for strength that I might achieve. But I was made weak, that I might learn to humbly obey.

I asked for health that I might do great things. I was given infirmity, that I might do better things.

I asked for riches that I might be happy. I was given poverty, that I might be wise.

I asked for power, that I might have the praise of men. I was given weakness so that I might feel the need of God.

I got none of the things I asked for, but I got a life that I might appreciate all things.

I am of all men, one of the most richly blessed."

From this wonderful, lofty viewpoint, please reassess how lucky you really are! You are not a victim at all. You are, in fact, the victor!

WHY BAD THINGS HAPPEN TO GOOD PEOPLE

Killer cyclone. Plane crash. Road accident. Murder. Hijacking. Embezzlement. Divorce. Result: loss of a loved one, permanent physical disability, paralysis, financial ruin, trauma, neurosis, death.

"Why? Why me?" sob the victims or the bereaved. "What have I done to deserve this?" During the Second World War a German soldier wrenched away a baby suckling at its Jewish mother's breast and before her very eyes threw it into the air, laughed and shot it with his revolver. The screaming mother looked into the sky with tears in her eyes and cried out, "Oh God! Where are you right now?"

These are moments of great trial for believers and atheists alike. Our angry, anguished minds demand a rational answer and our hearts a soothing, pacifying one. Nothing less than a massive paradigm shift can answer these perplexities and it will take great emotional courage and intellectual insight to comprehend and acknowledge. The essential truth is, we are not objective enough to realize that bad may also be good in the long term and good may turn out to be bad in the long term. Hitler's birth and childhood brought great joy to his mother, teachers and friends. He was "sunny, well turned out and companionable." But years later, this adorable child brought the end to six million Jews in Germany and 55 million people worldwide!

Please don't get me wrong. I don't mean to say all who die tragically are dormant monsters any more than all those who survive are necessarily angels. The point is, we simply don't know what is going to happen in the long term future. For instance, in anticipation of an Apollo 11 moon tragedy, an obituary speech for the astronauts had been prepared for US president Richard Nixon in advance! Even more pointedly, possibly 90% of major technologies today ranging from air and space travel, satellite television broadcasts and the Internet to IQ tests and weather warning systems actually had their origins or development in the military. Today, we feel glad and thank these scientific breakthroughs for their role in helping millions of people in the present and possibly billions of people in the future. In this light, were the First and Second World Wars bad for mankind or good? We cannot know for certain. Recently, for those lucky enough to be able to afford a plane trip from the US to Cairo on the ill-fated Egypt Air Flight 990 Boeing 767, it turned out their financial advantage and rendezvous with technology was 'bad'. "Superman" Christopher Reeves' stardom facilitated a rich lifestyle that took him horse-riding. The horse threw him: Superman became a paraplegic. Poor people die of malaria or other diseases easily curable by modern medicines. A lack of financial support may save one from a plane crash or horse-riding accident but not necessarily from malaria or malnutrition.

So the question is not really "Why me?" but "Why anybody?" and the answer lies in the simple truth: because of the way we think. We need to turn our scars into stars. Author Isabel Allende lost her young daughter, Paula, due to a mistake by medical personnel at a hospital where she had been admitted for a simple illness. Devastated, Allende considered committing suicide, suing the hospital or writing a book to heal herself. She chose the third! "I finally understood what life is about," she wrote. "It is about losing everything." Life is about celebrating what we have, while we have it. Just as the trees and plants blossom in season and later shed their leaves and flowers, similarly we humans arrive and depart when nature ordains. Allende's example and that of countless others demonstrate that what happens to us counts for little compared to how we react to what happens to us. Many celebrities or their spouses, children or friends leave behind or set up charitable foundations for the treatment and research of diseases such as cancer which they or their relatives had become victims of. The introspection and enlightenment of just one soul or family has the potential to help thousands, millions or even billions of people!

A priest and a parishioner saw a starving, helpless man collapsed by the roadway. Both looked up and prayed, "Oh, Lord! Don't you see this innocent soul? Are you not going to do anything for him?" Replied God, "I have seen him, I have – that's why I've sent you."

COMPULSIVE EXHIBITIONISTS

SELF IMPROVEMENT...

There are always some people around who seem to be compulsive exhibitionists. You can find them almost anywhere and they would do anything to get noticed. At a wedding they want to be the bride and at a funeral, the corpse! Julius Caesar – an incorrigible egoist – was once kidnapped in his younger years and held ransom for 12,000 gold pieces. Horrified he exhorted his captors to raise the ransom to 250,000 gold pieces so as to preserve his prestige!

Ostentation is the oxygen of our lives. Said English playwright William Shakespeare, "Praises are my wages." Said American writer Mark Twain, "I can live an entire week on compliments alone."

Rare are those souls who don't thrive on being the centre of attraction. They are the ones who are able to [illegible] their

COMPULSIVE EXHIBITIONISTS

There are always some people around who seem to be compulsive exhibitionists. You can find them almost anywhere; and they would do anything to get noticed. At a wedding they want to be the bride and at a funeral, the corpse! Julius Caesar – an incorrigible egotist – was once kidnapped in his younger years and held ransom for 11,000 gold pieces. Horrified, he exhorted his captors to raise the ransom to 250,000 gold pieces so as to preserve his prestige!

Ostentation is the oxygen of our lives. Said English playwright William Shakespeare, "Praises are my wages." Said American writer Mark Twain, "I can live an entire week on compliments alone."

Rare are those souls who don't thrive on being the centre of attraction. They are the ones who are able to derive their nourishment from within. They are the true giants of humanity; the others being no more than decorated dwarfs. It is said that a famous boxer once refused to tie his seatbelt aboard a plane. "Superman doesn't need a belt," he resisted. Tying his belt for him, the airhostess replied, "Superman doesn't need a plane either."

The truly great are those who know their own weaknesses and aren't afraid to admit them. They accept their limitations and blend with the crowd. When it comes to pure basics, they know everyone's the same. Beneath the Rolex watches and tattered clothes - rich and poor alike - American, Afghan or Indian - all have the same emotions deep inside: to protect their family, educate their children, provide for healthcare, to be free to walk the streets in safety, to have time for self, to contribute to the good of the world and to leave one's mark - however small - in its history. And the last is something all human beings do - for better or worse. Even an ant does not go through this world without creating its outcome in some way.

From the worldly perspective, humility can be imbibed by realizing the fact that the population of the planet is 6 billion people. When there was only one person on earth he had all rights of law, legislation, amendments and ownership. But after there came to exist two, then three, then four people, he was totally dethroned and his rights became one-fourth. Today, 6 billion people share equal rights - that is just one six billionth or 0.000000000166% rights per person! Yet, unable to come to terms with this reality, some people behave as though they are the owners of the planet. They are unable to take a back seat in any subject. They demand to be consulted before any decisions are made. They demand to be glorified and welcomed at every meeting. Most of the problems in this world are due to these people who yearn to feel important. To sustain their narcissistic beliefs they are prepared to kill, maim or degrade others under any banner or guise: religion, country or justice. In scaled-down versions, these self-initiated gods do the same thing in their own houses, to their own spouse, children, relatives and friends – all just to fulfil their grandiose fantasies about themselves!

God-consciousness however, is the elixir of egomania. Explains Bhagwan Swaminarayan in His Vachanamrut sermons, "When one realizes the infinite greatness and glory of God, where is there room for self-pride?" King Canute, who ruled England between 1016 and 1035, one day placed his golden throne on the sands of the seashore. He took his position on his throne and waited for the tide to come in. Eventually it did and wetted his feet. He repeatedly ordered the tide to go back, but it didn't. In fact, it returned with greater force and overturned his throne. Canute threw off his crown and never wore it again. He declared to the people, "Only by whose nod the heaven, earth and sea obeys laws eternal should be called King." With God-consciousness, we-all-go.

ETHICS AND DESIRES

Common-sense ethics must come before all else. Be it business, career or country. Loyalty to one's words. Determination to fulfil promises. Gratefulness for favours done for one. All this matters. It is what makes one trustworthy. It is what makes political leaders – and ordinary men and women great – more than looks, wealth, status and power. The latter are nice to have, but they can work well only in the hands of those with strong, ethical standards. It's the difference between a razor sharp scalpel in the hands of a great surgeon and the same instrument in the grip of a scheming thug. Said Greek philosopher Aristotle, "With morals Man is greater than an animal. But Man without morals is lower than an animal."

The reason behind this lower-than-Dr. Jekyll and Mr. Hyde duality is man's prodigious intellect. It allows him to talk straight or to lie. To let live or to let die. To rescue or to murder. God has bequeathed each of us with this specialized tool so that we can negotiate for the ethical and material betterment of everyone in the world – not just our own country, homes or selves. This intellect – if utilized correctly – will enable all of us to navigate our lives towards the maximum possible fulfilment of our souls' desires. But in parallel, the intellect should also be utilized for the attainment of spiritual enlightenment and salvation. Says the Shrimad Bhagwat, "God has created the mind, intellect and body for the purpose of sensual gratification and also spiritual salvation." Says Bhagwan Swaminarayan in His Shikshapatri, "They who live within the constraints of this Patri will attain to righteousness, wealth, the fulfilment of their desires and also to the attainment of spiritual liberation."

Deep desires and ambitions are not harmful if they are guided and constrained by spiritual parameters. In fact, the intellect and the heart's desires are complementary. Therefore they must ride in tandem. The desires are the pedals and wheels. The intellect, the steering and brakes. Only 1% of the problems of the world are due to natural disasters. Ninety-nine percent are due to people not using their intellect. Even those individuals who seem to benefit from their unethical activities pay dearly – spiritually, certainly – but also physically and psychologically. You see, even if you win the rat race (it is difficult to win without being unethical), you are still a rat! In fact, you are probably a fully-grown one. It is a fact not to be doubted that those who live unethically – beneath their flashy cars, gold watches and plastic smiles – lies a deeply broken man or woman. A person perpetually anxious of his safety. Forever worried about his or her future. Incessantly fighting with their inner voice. At night they have nightmares of the people they have hurt arriving to murder them. Many scream in their sleep, awaking in a cold sweat. To be sure, the picture is not pretty for the victims of their abominations, either. But indubitably, the softest and most comfy pillow when you sleep at night is a clear conscience. What can beat that?

HOW TO MOTIVATE YOUR MIND

There's no limit to the number of things a person can achieve in his or her lifetime. And it doesn't have to be at the expense of one's career, family, health and religious life. This might sound like an exaggeration, but everything that is really worth achieving can be achieved whilst maintaining an almost perfect balance with everything else. One can still become a tycoon and be a family man or woman, enjoy good health and be intensely religious – altogether.

But a human being cannot perform even the most simplest of tasks if he or she lacks just one thing: motivation. Just as a car cannot move without fuel in its tanks and a fan cannot spin without electricity flowing through its wires, similarly, bereft of motivation, a mind cannot inspire a person to action. Bereft of this psychological driving force, though people have an idea of what they want in their lives, they are just too confused, lethargic or depressed to pursue their aspirations. Many parents wonder why their children are not putting as much time as they obviously should into their studies. Many married couples wonder why their spouses are not doing more to get ahead in their lives though they have ample time and opportunity. The reason is not always that these children and grownups are just plain lazy or stubborn but sometimes simply because their minds lack the crucial ingredient of motivation.

People can be divided into two categories: pleasure-seekers and pain-avoiders. Pain-avoiders are not highly obsessed with begetting pleasure and delights. They are content in simply avoiding distressing situations. So it would be no good to regularly tell your indolent or indifferent child if he or she is a pain-avoider, that if he or she does not work hard at studies, he or she will not be able to earn lots and lots of money and buy lots and lots of goodies. He doesn't care about goodies. She doesn't care for money. What they want to do is avoid pain. As simple as that! What you have to explain and remind such a child frequently to get him or her motivated is, "If you don't study, people will hurt you because you will not have a good education. They will deceive you and take away whatever you have earned through your hard work. You will be miserable and helpless since you will have no standing in society." Use a similar strategy to motivate yourself; first introspect and identify which of the above two categories of people you belong to. Once this is done, follow the same type of arguments to infuse and imbue your mind with the will and energy to get up and do whatever you have to do to achieve your goals.

Contemplate upon the pains or pleasures that will result from your doing or not doing what you need to do. Try to conjure up in your mind a live and vivid image in full colour of all the sweet and bitter consequences. The image should include all the sights, smells, tastes, sounds, sensations and emotions – positive or negative – that you will experience if you do not do what you need to do: vivid images about the future have a tremendous capacity to awake a person to action. Then note down a full description of all these scenes and remind yourself of them by reading through them everyday.

In 1953, Yale University conducted a study of 1,500 boys and girls in Class 10. They were asked to write on a piece of paper what they wanted to do and become when they grew up. In 1973, Yale students tracked down these people to assess their achievements in comparison with the goals they had written down 20 years earlier. They found that the students who had written down their goals in vivid detail only 3 percent of them were so successful that they were earning more money than the other 97 percent put together!

But remember, the secret of happiness is balance. A lop-sided life – like a four-legged table standing on only three legs – will rock continuously and precariously. Fending the problems and exigencies of life effectively is quite impossible without the complete social, familial and spiritual infrastructure to do it. So decide and visualize four dreams; what you will do for yourself, your family, society and God. You should try to pursue all four goals simultaneously, rather than in succession. Time – nor anything else – is going to wait for you. You must tend to all your duties together.

HOW TO TAKE CHARGE OF YOUR LIFE

Freedom or independence has been the most frequent cause for which millions of people have laid down their lives in countless civil and international conflicts throughout history. "Democracy" has become the buzzword of the Western world since the defeat of communism in Russia and countries such as China and today, Pakistan, are being put under increasing pressure to adopt a more democratic system of government.

Ironically, people living in so called democratic states, continue to feel they are not yet quite in charge of their lives! They have to dance to the tune of somebody else's song, render lip service to somebody else's hero, pursue the career of somebody else's choice, wear the clothes of somebody else's approval and act in accordance with somebody else's ideals or value system! These people don't live in true freedom but in subservience to some home brewed concoction of ideas and fantasies of their associates, who in turn received their ideas from the usually superficial and frivolous media – as do people living in materialistic countries such as the United States and in Europe. Said Leon Wieseltier, cultural editor of the *New Republic*, "Hollywood is significantly responsible for the infantilisation of America."

Liberating the mind from the prison of peer pressure and public opinion is a crucial step in the crusade for true independence. People are more prisoners of their own psyches, than of society or the State. Psychologists call this 'Learned Helplessness'. In an experiment, a raccoon was strapped down tightly in a metal cage with a rubber ball at one end and a small electrical current was applied to the cage. The raccoon attempted to pounce upon the ball, presuming it was the cause of its pain, but couldn't. The experiment was repeated several times and the raccoon soon gave up even trying to pounce on the ball. The amazing thing was, even after the straps were removed and administering small electrical shocks was resumed, the raccoon continued to accept its suffering, lying down without making any attempt to pounce on the ball whatsoever! Many humans too, continue to passively accept being buffeted around by social pressures, instead of realizing they are always free to react – or not to react – if they choose.

To emulate or abide by what we know deep down to be a falsehood is the severest and saddest form of slavery. Many Germans – intellectuals, scientists, artists, laymen and soldiers alike – followed in the footsteps of Adolph Hitler, knowing fully that his philosophy was wrong. Independence and total responsibility for one's own actions and character was opined by one of the most progressive minded and influential spiritual leaders of this millennium – Bhagwan Swaminarayan. Said Indian historian Dr. N.A. Thoothi in his book *Vaishnavas of Gujarat* about Mahatma Gandhi, who was named Person of the Century by *The Times of India* and Runner up by *Time International* magazine, "In spite of his considerable indebtedness to Western thought and method, Mahatma Gandhi is perhaps most influenced in his inner most being by the teachings of Hinduism in general, and by the teachings and activities of the Swaminarayan Sampradaya sect above all." Bhagwan Swaminarayan explained to the masses that a true spiritual leader would never instruct men and women to pursue an immoral path. If by chance he does, a person should understand that God is putting him or her through the ultimate character test – and they must not flinch from their morality. For instance, a rich and learned man approached a Guru for a revelation. The Guru advised him he should stand in the centre of the City Square when it was pouring with rain, with his arms stretched towards the clouds. He did precisely as he was told and returned to the teacher. "I felt like a fool," he said. "I told you that you would have a revelation," replied the Master.

Respect your judgment, decide your goal, tread your chosen path. Listen to that faint inner voice within your deepest conscience. Try to follow it. Remain sane in the midst of insanity and take charge of your life!

THE TRUE BEAUTY CONTEST

Beauty contests are a blow to the integrity and intelligence of our women. External appearances will fade in just a few years; only internal beauty lasts after the wrinkles and varicose veins arrive. And only her character will survive in the hearts of the people after her body has been consigned to the earth or flames. The greatest women this world has seen are not remembered for their physical beauty – such as Florence Nightingale, Rosa Parks, Helen Keller, Ahilyabai Holkar, Jhansiki Rani Laxmibai, Sarojini Naidu and others. In fact, the more beautiful and glitzy women have become, the more we see their souls were empty, their bodies as mere carcasses – devoid of self-esteem – and sometimes depressed to the point of committing suicide: Marilyn Monroe. Let this so-called icon be an example to all the women of India and the rest of the world of the consequences of exulting and pursuing pure beauty alone.

Another reality is the simple fact that most people are never going to be as good looking as the male and female specimens we call "Miss World" and "Mr. Universe". So why create stress and anxiety in the masses by telling them, albeit indirectly – through these beauty contests – that they're deficient in their appearance? Conveying these messages makes them feel inferior for the rest of their lives and because they lose their self-confidence it affects their academic and creative performance, too. In a recent study conducted by University of Sussex psychologist Rob Bracey, it was found that girls who wore provocative clothing scored lower in IQ tests compared to their classmates simply because such girls are almost always engrossed in monitoring how others are looking at them, rather than concentrating on their studies. "A woman wearing a bikini simply can't think straight," he says. "If you are wearing skimpy swimwear, then part of your brain is continuously monitoring everyone else around you... she can't concentrate on other things. If she goes back to the office (wearing full clothing) she may feel the effect for hours or even days. It's quite basic psychology." Similar effects would be experienced by males working close to these women. As a result, neither are able to apply their minds fully to their work and achieve anything really outstanding in their careers.

Lastly, if these so-called beauty queens are Cinderellas, are all other females in the world ugly sisters? Certainly not. The real truth is that there is only one beautiful or handsome child in the world – and every mother has it! Everyone is beautiful. Every human being is a masterpiece. Even if that person is disabled or deformed, obese or has discoloured skin, because he or she still possesses a human body! If these people are given the right encouragement and inspiration, all of them can work miracles with their bodies. Bhagwan Swaminarayan explains in His Vachanamrut sermons, "What is unattainable with this human body? Anything and everything can be achieved if one has regularity and perseverance." Have we not seen people who are almost totally paralyzed drawing beautiful paintings with a paintbrush held between their teeth or between their toes? Do we not listen to the music of maestros like Beethoven who was stone deaf and read the books of Helen Keller who was both deaf and blind? Do we not see the improvement in IQ of mentally handicapped boys and girls who are given unceasing encouragement and love from their devoted parents?

It is said that one mother is equal to a hundred good teachers. It is therefore the duty of all parents to sit with their siblings and explain the falsehood behind the media giving so much emphasis to good looks in advertisements, films and beauty contests. We all need to open our eyes to the fact that true beauty lies in doing beautiful things.

RETURN TO GOODNESS, NOT FAIRNESS

Did you know that thousands of years ago, an ancient Chinese king developed a liking for plump women and filled his entire palace with them? The amazing thing is that soon after, it became prestigious to be fat and every woman in the land was clambering to add on an extra 20 kilos! Fat was glamorous, plump was beautiful, large was attractive. And those who were thin became low, cheap and repulsive.

Similarly, today in the 21st Century, if all those who have fair skin are to be considered beautiful, the whole of Europe, Russia, America and China should be hailed as beauty pageants and the whole of Africa and Jamaica be denounced as halls of horror. This is the unavoidable conclusion if we are to accept the "Return To Fairness" advertisements and others like it that we are surrounded by everywhere.

Such misleading advertisements rot the superb moral and intellectual fibres of our history, culture and ideals. The father of our nation – Mahatma Gandhi – can be considered as the epitome of all that is truly Indian. Churchill feared him, Mussolini respected him and Einstein revered him. However, please note: Gandhiji was dark in colour and wore simple clothes. Bhagwan Swaminarayan was dark too, so was Shri Krishna and Shivji. Many of the greatest citizens, saints and avatars of our country were dark. And great women such as Ahilyabai Holkar, Jhansiki Rani Laxmibai and Sarojini Naidu of India and Rosa Parks of the black freedom movement in America are not remembered for their physical beauty but for the beautiful works they did. Those wonderful women are still adored today.

So why must we Indians pursue fairness? What is so grand

or elevated about it? And why worry about something that is not going to change? If your father is dark, your mother is dark and if you love your mother and father and all the other great dark heroes of India, why should you want to be anything other than dark? Be proud to be dark! It's your heritage and your inheritance. While in Western lands people are trying to get a dark tan and look like the average Indian, we over here are using sunscreens to look like the average European! What a joke! Girls and boys in India have become so obsessed with looking white, they are spending thousands of rupees on dubious soaps and creams. Abroad, girls and boys are contracting skin cancer trying to get a dark tan.

Be proud to be Indian! Every sixth person in the world is an Indian! And all that is truly Indian is beautiful. Whether it be dark or fair – if it represents our eternal ideals, be proud of it. But worrying over one's complexion is frivolous and wastes far too much time, effort and thinking on the part of those caught in its web. India needs to restore and reinforce the self-confidence and self-esteem of its people. A student who is fretting over his or her complexion will hardly be able to concentrate at school or college or in the home; nor could that citizen become a fully attentive mother or father after marriage.

In India we are increasingly swallowing whole, without any independent thinking, what money-minded film-producers, beauty contest organizers and cosmetic firms want us to believe. In almost all our movies and advertisements the heroes and heroines are portrayed to have fair skin and villains as dark or obese! This is simply not true to life! In reality, "good looking" people are not necessarily good people and "ugly" people are not necessarily bad, either. That's precisely why marriages based solely on physical attraction almost always end up in divorce. And have you ever considered how people in Africa and the Adivasi areas of India must marry each other and love each other and their children despite their large lips, protruding teeth and flat faces? It's because they have not been brainwashed by the media!

Throw fairness soaps out of the window. Let us 'Return to Goodness' instead.

TAKE RESPONSIBILITY FOR YOUR LIFE AND ACTIONS

One of the most difficult and painful things to do in life is to admit the mistakes and blunders one has made. When Neil Armstrong set foot on the moon he was supposed to say, "That's a small step for a man, but a giant leap for mankind". But he erred. What he actually said was, "That's a small step for man, but a giant leap for mankind." The words exist in recording and millions of people heard the goof up. But, to this very day, he maintains he uttered the correct version!

The hesitation in confessing one's mistakes, express one's regrets, make amendments or simply give a heartfelt apology is at the root of much strife amidst individuals, within families and between nations today. It's not always that people don't want to forgive, but that people don't want to ask forgiveness and admit they wronged. Said twice Pulitzer Prize winner and celebrated historian Barbara Tuchman when reporters asked her what she thought was most needed in the next century: "Personal Responsibility – taking responsibility for one's behaviour and not forever supposing that society must forgive you because it's not one's fault." The fault may not be totally one's own. But usually, in some subtle way – either through action, reaction or even inaction – we played our role poorly or maladroitly.

A teenager had just passed his driving test and was eager to drive his father's car. His father agreed on the condition that he should drop him at a place about 18 miles from home and then take the car for servicing. The boy should then come back in the afternoon at 4 p.m., pick him up and they would go home together. The boy dropped off his father, took the car to the garage and promptly went to watch a film. Not realizing how much time had elapsed, the boy continued to watch the film until 6 p.m. Afraid his father would scold him for being late and would never give him the car again, he collected the car, arrived at the appointed place and said, "Dad, I'm sorry I'm late but it took the mechanic longer to service the car than usual." "Son. I phoned the garage," His father replied. "The car was ready at 4 p.m." The boy looked down. "I'm sorry, but I went to watch a film." "Son, I'm very angry," replied the father after a moment of thought. "But not with you. I'm angry with myself. Where did I go wrong all these years as a father that my own son is unable to confide in me honestly? You take the car home. I will walk back and introspect for the whole journey." His son tailed behind pleading with his father to sit inside the car. But his father continued walking silently and introspecting all the way back home – all 18 miles. From that day onwards the boy pledged in his mind he would never again tell a lie to his parents.

What a wonderful story! Not only has the boy been transformed, so has the father! This is what the world needs more of. We all have to look into ourselves – where we have gone wrong. Not where others have gone wrong. We cannot change others. We can only change ourselves. And if we all decided to do just that, then there would be no need to change anybody else anyway. The world would be transformed in a single blow.

Another thing which needs transforming is the negative way in which almost everyone interprets their lives. Everyone thinks they are burdened with unending problems. No one seems to be truly happy. Even the rich, famous and powerful hide depression and frustration beneath their makeup and plastic smiles. This is why even these people are known to have thrown it all away by committing suicide: Elvis Presley, Marilyn Monroe, Vincent Foster, Guru Dutta Padukone and hundreds of thousands of lesser known people throughout the world every year!

Try to change your attitude towards "problems". Problems are not problems at all. Your circumstances can be viewed very positively if you wish. You're only making them appear to be negative – by using negative terminology such as 'embarrassment', 'hardship', 'burden' and 'ordeal'. They are really 'revelations' 'duties', 'responsibilities', 'labours of love', 'missions', 'loyalties', 'challenges' and 'opportunities'. The words you use generate mindsets in you. Viewing everything positively will help you to grow and create the skill and ability that will shape your life – and our world – more than you can ever dream.

ART OF BECOMING A GENIUS

Throughout history, the world has been witness to a great galaxy of geniuses from every domain. From physics we had Einstein, from technology we had Edison, from arts we had Michelangelo, from grammar we had Panini, and from mathematics we had Ramanujan. Though all of these prodigies hailed from differing fields, if we look carefully, we will find they all had one thing in common – not an exceptionally high IQ but a profound, unconditional love for their subjects.

Students always come to me asking how they can improve their memory and concentration. I always ask them how they manage to remember cricket scores from ten years earlier if they didn't have a memory or the ability to concentrate?

Frankly, God has already endowed us with all the faculties we need to study well and do wonderful things. My message to students is this: if you are finding a subject tough, or if you are having difficulty concentrating, the reason is you are, probably, not giving that subject your unconditional love. This may seem new to some, but just think. If you were to fire a gun at a thick lead wall, you would not expect the bullets to pierce through it. Similarly, despite heavy reading and long hours, if your brain is unable to register any information, you probably have some sort of mental barricade obstructing the passage of information from your eyes (or ears) to your brain! That barrier must be razed to the ground. The barrier consists of your negative attitude towards the subject. You are not sufficiently interested in it. You have no real appreciation of its value and you view it as a burden. All you want is to exploit it for marks. If this is your attitude, the subject will not open up to you and your books will remain as good as

closed. A book is not just a piece of paper it is almost like a living person, wishing to speak to you. If he (or she) feels you are not interested, he or she will remain silent. Would you open your heart and innermost sanctum to a person who does not care for you or just wants to use you?

But what if a person gives you unconditional love? Then, you would open your heart to him or her and reveal all you know and all your secrets and troubles! Similarly, if you give your unconditional love to your difficult subjects, you will find they begin to open up to you just as at the break of dawn, a rose opens to the bees and butterflies who come to collect nectar from its depths! You will feel relieved of that tiresome burden of studying which will metamorphose into an experience of freshness and eagerness. The subjects you were struggling with will suddenly become simple and straightforward. Most of all, you will find you have to make no more efforts to concentrate and very little effort to memorize!

Thus, students who sincerely want to be more successful should strive to personify their subjects and treat them like actual people! They should treat their books with respect and kindness. The books should be held lovingly and placed gently and reverently on tables not flung onto the floor or bed. The student should try to become intimate with the subject or book he wishes to study and say, "Listen, I really want to learn more about you and get to know you better. And, I want you to know that I don't care what others say about you. Whatever your deficiencies, I still love you! And even after the examinations are over and whatever marks I get I will still value you."

Try it! There is no subject that is difficult to memorize or concentrate upon if you love it. So give your unconditional love! At first it may be difficult, but keep trying. Gradually, it will not only better your grades it will transform your whole life, because it will train you in a new habit. It will teach you to become a mother and caregiver to all beings and all things. And throughout your life, in whatever you do and in whichever vocation you are, you will feel connected and immensely happy and it will give you a great sense of job satisfaction, as well.

ART OF SOCRATIC STUDY

"No doubt is a silly doubt," proclaimed Albert Einstein. "If a man will begin with certainties, he shall end in doubts; but if he will be content to begin with doubts, he shall end with certainties," expounded Sir Francis Bacon.

Doubting is the first step to true knowledge, to deep conviction. Doubting forces a person to ponder thoughtfully on the subject on which he or she is unclear and pinpoints to both student and mentor the area of ignorance that needs enlightening. It spurs the student to go deeper and often beyond the usual area of study to understand broader, deeper and more philosophical, psychological and historical fundamentals. Doubting means asking successively or in any order the questions: Who? What? Which? Where? Why? When? And How? They lead to amazing insights about things that would normally have been taken for granted and also adds fun and joy to learning. This method, used thousands of years ago in India and Europe, is known as the "Socratic Method".

Some examples.

In mathematics, you may ask, "How do you know whether x should go below y or above it?" "How do you decide which process of calculation – addition, subtraction, multiplication or division – needs to be performed?" Indeed, "How do you know there is a process to be performed at all?" These may sound like simple questions, but they are fundamental. If you master the solutions to these simple questions, your mathematical prowess will be insuperable.

Therefore, ask basic, fundamental questions. Ignore what people might say of you when they hear them: remember, the only dumb question is the one that was not asked. But the problem today is that pupils are overly afraid their peers or teachers might belittle them and teachers are afraid students will embarrass them. "Aristotle was the Father of Philosophy," announced a teacher. "Any questions?" "Who was the Mother of Philosophy?" asked a smart alec. "Mrs. Aristotle," replied the quick teacher. Other teachers may not be so adept. In a biology class, a teacher immersed an earthworm in a beaker of clear alcohol. Within a few minutes, it had totally dissolved. "Voila!" said the teacher triumphantly. "Now tell me what happens to your intestines when you drink alcohol." "All the worms get cleared out," someone replied from the back of the class. Everyone roared.

What's wrong with laughing at a good joke? It makes learning and teaching far lighter. It takes the strain out of studying and provides a more conducive atmosphere to true learning rather than rote learning. A boring board meeting, a tension-filled emergency or an anxiety-creating examination could all do with a momentary burst of laughter. It makes you breathe deeper, release the tension and explode away your negative mindsets.

Learn to ask questions. It sharpens your intellect and clarifies your perceptions. It lifts the fog and helps you see the day. The joy of knowledge is in the understanding. The experience is a form of enlightenment - a material enlightenment that touches on the borders of the spiritual. It's a brief taste of omniscience. Intoxicating, exhilarating and pacifying - all in the same breath.

But please don't take this message as true for granted. Challenge it. Counter it. Come to terms with it only after having analyzed it thoroughly. This is the ancient, time-tested road to the realization of genuine truth. But avoid becoming an inveterate agnostic. Not all questions will have answers. Some need to be solved within one's brain, others within one's heart. Some answers can be verbalized or symbolized. Others are beyond all such tools and ironically, are usually the only ones that really matter.

MAGICAL POWER OF DREAMING

Anthropologists maintain that human beings have possessed a fully developed brain for at least the past 25,000 years. How is it then, that we have begun to progress technologically only since the last two hundred years? What were we doing till now? For eons we gazed and wondered at the stars. For eons we enviously watched the birds fly and the fish frolicking beneath the ocean surface and for eons we looked in awe at bursting and dazzling flashes of lightning amongst the dark and misty clouds. Yet man only looked – he did not dream! He had underestimated his capabilities. Worse, he had overestimated his limitations. For millennia, our ancestors abandoned brilliant ideas, penetrating insights and fresh possibilities. They could not conceive, therefore they could not create.

Today, we know that nothing is impossible in this world. If it can be dreamt, it can be achieved. We shall see but five examples out of literally thousands of instances of man's genius and dexterity in forging methods that make the impossible become possible!

1. Till 1879, scientists believed it was impossible to invent an incandescent electric light bulb. And indeed, Thomas A.

Edison's several thousand attempts to invent one had all met with total failure. Nobody believed it was possible - except Edison - who faithfully continued to conduct experiment after experiment. Upon his announcement that he had finally succeeded, many scientists jeered in disbelief. One respected specialist in arc lighting - Edwin Western, proclaimed that Edison's assertion was "so manifestly absurd as to indicate a positive want of knowledge of the electric circuit." But seeing was believing and ultimately all had to bow before Edison's now legendary story of success. Edison's persistent pursuit of an inner dream made possible an invention that would ultimately throw light into billions of homes and offices around the world!

2. Since the 1850s, the U.S. military had been trying to invent an airplane - a "flying machine" - because its possession would be a decisive factor in times of war. However, they finally gave up hope on two grounds. For one, theory said it was impossible for pilots to breathe at speeds greater than 60 miles per hour and secondly, scientists were proclaiming that heavier-than-air flying machines were "utterly impossible". However, two amateur engineers - Orville and Wilbur Wright - continued to pursue their dream of one day flying in the sky along with the birds! Ultimately, to the embarrassment and envy of the U.S. military, in 1903 near Kitty Hawk, North Carolina, they became the first human beings in engine-powered flight - showing the world yet again that there is no limit to what mankind can do.
3. In 1957, Britain's Astronomer Royal - Sir Harold Spencer Jones, declared to the world with considerable scientific clout, "Space travel is bunk." However, just two weeks later, the Russians successfully launched the first space rocket - the spectacular Sputnik 1 into orbit around the Earth!
4. In the second century B.C.E a young Indian boy of age 7 was

told by an astrologer peering at his hand that he did not have the required lines of education to become a scholar. The young boy went into the house, brought out a knife, drew it where the line should have been and asked the astrologer, "Now can you see the line?" The boy was Panini, who grew to become one of the greatest grammarians in the history of Sanskrit – making it so perfect that Forbes Magazine nominated it as the most computer compatible language in the world!

Every human being has a special, deep-seated dream – it may be to become a millionaire, a great scientist, artist, actor, inventor, leader, philanthropist or crusader for human rights – anything whatsoever. The message to all these dreamers is, whatever your dream – everything is possible – if you believe in yourself. God has already endowed you with everything you need to achieve your dreams. You have a human body, which has an incredible capacity for versatility, adaptability and creativity. Utilize your God-given resources and live life to your fullest and finest potential. Bequeath the world a new invention, a work of art or a beautiful thought. Remember: What you are, is God's gift to you. What you become, is your gift to God – and to the world.

REWARDS OF CONTROLLING YOUR EMOTIONS

"Do you exercise, sir?" asked the fitness supporter. "Yes," replied the man. "I exercise restraint."

To lead a healthy and successful life it is of great necessity that we learn to control our emotions. Anger, lust, greed and jealousy are temporary madnesses. They are akin to hijackers and are dangerous companions to travel with. Many people suffer from emotional hijackings several times a day. These emotions may last for only a few minutes or even moments. But they can ruin a career, devastate a marriage or end a life. The majority of people in jail around the world are there not because of long careers of criminality but fleeting moments of such emotional madness.

If you list all your most unpleasant memories you will find that at the root of most of them is a form of humiliation – a failure, a defeat, an injustice – culminating in a sense of lowered self-esteem. It is usually these negative experiences which have fueled your negative emotions and actions as a form of coping strategy. But such methods are self-defeating and ultimately serve only to exacerbate one's problems as it does when a person takes to drugs, alcohol or smoking to overcome tensions or anxieties. We can't change the past; but we can change our response and attitude towards it. And in doing so we can also improve our present and future.

In his book *Emotional Intelligence: How It Can Matter More Than IQ,* Daniel Goleman describes a study conducted in the 1960s at Stanford University of the children of its own faculty members. The children studied were all of age 4. They were offered one sweet immediately or two sweets if they were prepared to wait 20 minutes. Thirty-three percent of them demanded the single sweet immediately. The children were traced 12-14 years later and it was found that those who had resisted immediate gratification by waiting 20 minutes (which must seem like ages for a child), were more socially competent, self-assertive and able to cope with the frustrations of life. They were more self reliant, trustworthy and plunged into projects.

Everyone has emotions. After all, we are all humans. But the task is to learn how to express one's feelings in an acceptable way. In the 1970s, 250 executives in the US were interviewed. Most said their vocation demanded hard-headedness, not sentimentality. Today, the tables have turned. Good, clear, sensitive and appreciative two-way feedback is required. When feedback is not given, negative feelings build up and may later explode. Sometimes silence, though well intentioned, becomes the source of confusion, suspicion and accusation.

A good guideline in developing better relationships with people is to first ask yourself how you would like to be treated if you were on the other end of the stick. Introspect and reflect on how in some similar way, you too have been guilty of similar mistakes. We need to learn to empathize with other people – to recognize that the pain we induce in their lives due to our words, actions or inaction is real. If you can feel his or her pain yourself, you will be loathe to carry through with the action. Such an internal transformation may seem like a weakness to some – a form of accepting defeat or failure. But in his best selling book *The Seven Habits of Highly Effective People* Stephen S. Covey describes it as "Win/Win". Everyone gains – emotionally, physically (health), socially and spiritually! "Saintly knowledge brings happiness to both the possessor and the people he or she lives with," explains His Divine Holiness Pramukh Swami Maharaj. "A demonic mannerism brings only misery to the people who possess it and the people they live with."

A man waited furiously for his regular tutti-frutti ice cream at a restaurant, which was unable to offer the ice cream immediately. After 15 minutes the waiter produced it on his table. Eyeing it for a moment, the man swept it away on the floor. "I'll rather have my grievance," he said.

Deep down, doesn't this resemble the way many of us lead our lives? Only when we learn to vanquish our negative emotions will we be able to receive the rewards of life, keep them – and enjoy them.

THINGS ARE NOT WHAT THEY SEEM

If it looks like a duck, walks like a duck and quacks like a duck, it must be a duck. Seeing is believing. This is the maxim most people subscribe to. However today, psychologists have discovered that 90% of what we see actually lies behind our eyes. Our brain is a super computer processor, but it is often not super enough. Its function is to filter the barrage of continual information it receives flowing in from our eyes, ears, nose, tongue and skin, discarding or rejecting supposedly unimportant information such as a dog barking in the distance, somebody hammering nails in the wall next door or the change in illumination around us as the sun rises or sets or when clouds block its rays. In most of these highly varying situations, we notice little and continue on our way as though nothing has changed.

This ability of the brain is for the most part a highly desirable feature or else a person would go simply mad from the onslaught of stimuli around him, unable to focus on a single task, paralyzed between deciding which information to react to. In the 1920s, a Russian newspaper reporter named Solomon Shereshevskii could recall every minute of his life in detail! He could remember seventy numbers in any order even after fifteen years and could even recall the face of his mother looking into his crib when he was just one year old! He later became a professional mnemonist, but due to the enormous data mounting in his brain he became more and more confused as time went on and unable to lead a normal life.

Another uncanny ability of the mind is its capacity to synthesize images of objects that aren't actually there, such as when one watches a two dimensional image of an object or person on a movie screen and becomes as stirred or stimulated as though one is witnessing the real thing, in real life. If, however, the process of such holistic synthesis goes into aberrance, an otherwise healthy mind may perceive something "out there" that grossly and sometimes dangerously mismatches reality. A single part can create the wrong whole. This is apparent in rapists who attack their victims thinking they "asked for it" just because they were wearing a certain article of clothing, or murderers who attack their victims just because their skin colour matches that of other people they hate. Such sociopaths superimpose their distorted mindsets upon the neutral, contourless features of the innocent victim, thus creating in him or her what they consider to be "fair game".

The moth plunges suicidally into the vortex of the flame, the thirsty man scrambles towards the mirage of an oasis. The difference between an ordinary person and an enlightened saint is that the saint is continually awake to the illusions created by the mind. He laughs at the madhouse we live in with its billionaires begging, its fish thirsting and its immortal souls trembling in fear of death! As the Bhagvat Gita says, *"Yasyãm jãgarti bhutãni, sã nishã pashyato munehe."* – That in which deluded souls are active is seen as night by the awakened.

We live in a very subjective, self created world. This may be a disturbing revelation to some people, but subjectivity has great value too. It means every man or woman can pursue a different path to a similar goal or similar paths towards different goals, thus enabling more possibilities to be explored. It allows for multifarious creativity, culminating in the discoveries of scientific phenomena whose harnessing and understanding has allowed us to progress technologically in great leaps and bounds. It has also led to the field of arts – beautiful compositions by various maestros, paintings by artists, food by gourmets, books and plays by writers and playwrights. All this could not have come into existence if everyone had the same, objective view of the universe. In fact, man's genius lies in his ability to see things in a different way, in another light. But it can also spell his ruin, when he or she fails to understand the distinction between fantasy and reality which sometimes exists very differently from the way it is portrayed on the television, in the cinema or within the walls of one's skull. Such a blunder is qualitatively equivalent not only to misrecognizing a duck when one sees one but also to becoming one: quack, quack, quack.

YOU CAN CHANGE YOUR FATE!

Why do so few people achieve the deepest dreams of their childhood? Why do so many people end up saying, "If only my boss...", "If only my health...", "If only my luck..."? The answer is simple. They lack one thing: Passion.

In the 2 century B.C.E a young Indian boy of age 7 was told by an astrologer peering at his hand that he did not have the required lines of education on his palm to become a scholar. The young boy went into the house, brought out a knife, drew it where the line should have been and asked the astrologer, "Now can you see the line?" The boy was Panini, who grew to become one of the greatest grammarians in the history of Sanskrit.

In Hinduism, Karma theory is not a theory of bondage, as many construe, but liberation. As you sow, so shall you reap.

Imagine you are treading water at the centre of a flowing river. What is your destiny? Wherever the river ends up, of course. But what if you begin swimming towards either of the banks, or with greater effort, in the opposite direction against the current? Then almost any point along either bank of the entire river can become your destiny. You may even choose to step out of that river completely and walk upstream or plunge into an alternative river! Your fate is sealed only if you refuse to make any efforts to alter your course.

Bhagwan Swaminarayan repeats with emphasis many times in His Vachanamrut sermons that nothing is impossible with the human body if one is prepared to try hard enough, regularly enough and for long enough. It is here that the presence or absence of passion becomes the deciding factor. Passion is the substance that keeps people going, nourishing constant optimism,

despite formidable obstructions in their path.

In a US school, a child who had no steady education because he came from an extremely poor background was once asked by his schoolteacher to write an essay about what he wanted to do and become when he grew up. He spent hours writing through the night – longer than any of his classmates and also drew a map of a 200 acre ranch with race track and stables, etc. It also incorporated a detailed diagram of a 4,000 sq. ft. mansion, plus a swimming pool. A week later his teacher returned his work marked, "F. See me after class." He was shocked and heartbroken. "Why have you given me an F? This is my dream." The teacher explained, "Your essay isn't realistic. I want to save you from pain and frustration later in life. Write another essay and I'll give you a better grade." All night the boy struggled with the idea of changing or altering his dream to something else. The next day he returned to school and handed back the original essay. "Sir," he said, "You keep the F. I'm keeping my dream." That boy was none other than Marty Roberts who grew up to own a 200 acre ranch with 4,000 sq. ft. mansion – precisely as he had dreamed.

In 1953, Yale University conducted a study of 1,500 boys and girls in Class 10. They were asked to write on a piece of paper what they wanted to do and become when they grew up. In 1973, Yale students tracked down these people to assess their achievements in comparison with the goals they had written down 20 years earlier. They found that the students who had written down their goals in great detail, only 3 percent were so successful that they were earning more money than the other 97 percent put together!

Similar findings have been published in Daniel Goleman's best selling book *Emotional Intelligence: Why It Can Matter More Than IQ.* SAT scores have been found usually to contribute a maximum of only 20 percent to a person's final success. The other 80 percent is provided by one's EQ or "emotional quotient" which Goleman defines quite simply as one's personal character: qualities such as self restraint, empathy, friendliness and enthusiasm.

The Upanishads beseech, "Arise, awake and stop not till the goal is reached."

Become the sculptor of your own destiny. Trust yourself. Trust the sages. Trust God. The sky's the limit.

YOU GET FROM LIFE WHAT YOU GIVE TO IT

"Every action has an equal and opposite reaction," declared the great Isaac Newton in the 1700s. "Garbage in, garbage out" people say today – very much the same thing. Sow a seed, reap a fruit. Plant a chili, you get chilies back. Plant a mango, you get mangoes back. But how is it that sometimes people sow chilies but get mangoes and some sow mangoes but get chilies? This is not an inconsistency. The chilies are simply fruits of some earlier actions or decisions and the mangoes have yet to come. You can't force a seed to grow.

This is the natural law of the universe. You get what you give, though you may not recognize it because it may arrive earlier or later than you expected or in a somewhat different guise. We exhale and give carbon dioxide to plants and trees that metabolize it and release oxygen, which we metabolize and in turn return to the trees in the form of carbon dioxide. If we decide not to return carbon dioxide to the trees, slowly they will perish, and so will we. The cells in our body nourish one another, supporting and supplying each other with the nutrients the other lacks. It all goes to create the fabulous organic systems we call life.

If one befriends, one is befriended. If one loves, one is loved. One must not get dejected and stop sowing good seeds, because there exists no other way to receive good fruits. It's also worth remembering that frequently the bitter, drier fruits are more nutritious and healthy than the succulent, sweeter ones.

Love, family and friends enrich one's life more than any amount of wealth can. But one needs to make continual investments of friendliness, affection and love to keep the system fully charged. This is because we are all human beings and we simply don't love all the time. Sometimes we say nasty things to a loved one – something we don't really mean – but it amounts to a withdrawal from the love account. It needs to be redeposited as early as possible.

Affection and love are not about giving away money or buying expensive gifts all the time, though it is required on occasions. When you give your possessions, you give little. When you give yourself, you give it all. Time, a sympathetic ear, humour or a helping hand in times of distress are what more people need to receive and to give. It is human nature that we always seem to be convinced beyond all doubt that we give much more to society than we take or receive. Psychologists call it Self-Serving Bias: we have an unwitting capacity to forget our neighbour's good deeds, remember our good ones, and forget our bad ones! When taking turns to comfort and quiet a crying baby at night, husband and wife always seem to think that their turn comes more often than the other's. When going out for a treat, each member of a group thinks he or she always has to end up treating everyone else. In many instances this may be true. But when we consider the entirety of our lives, we have received in one way or another more than we have given (just ask your mum).

Giving also benefits your health. A 14-year study of 2700 people in Michigan State U.S. discovered that those who did voluntary charity work had longer life, were more free from heart disease, had lower blood pressure and more peace of mind.

The real magic of giving lies in the way you give: when planting your seeds, expect nothing in return. Give without remembering you gave and take without forgetting you took. Give with your whole being, your whole heart – remember, half a seed can't germinate.

The dynamics of happiness are asymmetrical. Fulfilment comes from giving, not receiving. The fact that so many people are still disappointed, frustrated and unfulfiled despite the fact they live in relative opulence compared to their forefathers is ample evidence they have only received. Said surgeon Dr. Doshi who has performed more than 100,000 operations for charity when asked what he got from it all, "A seven letter word." "Success?" somebody asked. "No," he replied "content".

Here lies the master formula for fulfilment: for getting – forgive and for giving – forget.

CULTURE...

BE PROUD OF INDIA!

"Mera Bharat Mahan!" – "My India is great." Is that truly so? What's so great about it? What with all the dust, mosquitoes, flies and a non-uniform civil code, who would ever conclude India to be a great or distinguished nation?

I would like to contradict. Despite all of this, India is still the most fabulous, enchanting and noble nation in the world. India is the country which has never stepped over its borders to invade another nation's territory. India is the country, 90% of whose citizens are pure vegetarians. India is the country whose citizens are the most freethinking in the world. India is the largest democracy in the world. India is self sufficient in food and defence. India is the country which with a simple strategy defeated a billion dollar US spy satellite lurking over its skies. India is the country which seduced an American President to its gates and is the country from whom the U.S., Germany and U.K. are importing thousands of skilled software engineers to boost their economies. India was the country that created the ingenious game of chess, originally known by the name of *gyaana baaji,* and she was the country that invented microsurgery. She was the country that discovered the fundamental and foundational concept required for computer programming – the "Zero" – which is used in the binary system (and is also the basis of the decimal system). Without the ingenious concept of Zero, computers today would not even exist. India was also the country that created Sanskrit – the language that Forbes magazine nominated as the most computer compatible language in the world. Through Sanskrit, India gave Europe all its languages – Latin, Greek, French, German, English, etc. – without which Plato,

Aristotle, Shakespeare, Emerson, Voltaire nor James Joyce could have written any of their masterpieces. India is the nation which bequeathed to the world ayurvedic medicines and yogic exercises which have proven immensely useful in the management of stress and anxiety, and the treatment of diseases. India is the country that gave birth to the great Mahatma Gandhi about whom Albert Einstein said, "Generations to come will scarce believe that such a one as this ever walked upon this earth." India is the only nation whose soldiers bury invading enemy soldiers killed in battle with full respects, tributes and in accordance with the religious beliefs of the enemy nation! India is the only land that can boast to be the host of every inspiration in the world!

Said U.S. historian Will Durant, "India was the motherland of our race... of the ideals embodied in Christianity... of self-government and democracy. In many ways, mother India is the mother of us all." Said U.S. poet and journalist J. Miller, "In those ancient days, even China had not worked it all out practically, and even Egypt inherited much of its sacred knowledge from India, subsequently to pass it on to Greece and then Europe still sunk in sleep. India held the palm of civilization and soon spread it all around her."

Despite all this, it is a pity that many Indians feel proud of their country only when it is praised by people in the West. These Indians lack faith not in the nation, but in themselves. The simple reason behind this is a dire lack of knowledge. Enlightenment makes us proud; ignorance makes us inferior. All that Indians lack is the will to believe in themselves and the courage to assert their own potential and capacities.

The glory of India is eternal. Let every Indian arise like the morning Sun to proudly spread and uphold India's goodness, culture and wisdom in their own hearts and throughout the world.

INDIA'S TRUE HEROES

During the Kargil conflict, the body of a downed fighter pilot lay in ceremony. His young widowed wife sat close by looking at him, her eyes veiled in a curtain of tears. Slowly a tear began to trickle down her cheek. Her young son of about eight years of age, sitting in her lap, put his finger on her lips and said forbiddingly, "Mummy, please don't cry. Daddy lost his life in a good cause."

Recently we read of Captain R. Subramaniam who was killed as he courageously pursued infiltrating gangs in Northern Kashmir. We also heard of three Majors – Major B.S. Bajwa, Major Sanjay Sood, Major P.R. Tathwade and seven other soldiers also laying down their lives for our country.

All these young men and numerous other soldiers fighting at our borders, their parents, wives and children are the true heroes and heroines of Mother India or Bharat Varsh. They are the people who are keeping this country afloat by their commitment and personal sacrifice. They are the people who are making India a better and safer place to live in for all of us presently and for all our grandchildren in the future.

Yet we forget these fabulous heroes all too easily and quickly revert to paying homage to false heroes such as sportsmen, actors and models who take from society a million-fold more than they give. Yet, we stick their pictures upon the walls of our homes and talk about them throughout the day. How many citizens of India pinned up on the walls and doors of their homes cuttings from magazines and newspapers depicting photographs of our soldiers braving the bitter conditions of Kargil, preparing to lose their lives so that we could keep ours? It

is only because of these brave *jawans* that we live in safety, free of anxiety in our cozy cities, well removed from the horrendous obscenities of war. Some of our *jawans* who got captured by the enemy were tortured, had their limbs chopped off and their eyes gouged out. How can we forget these celebrated people, India's genuine heroes? In fact, any individual who is doing something selflessly for the country and its citizens, giving their all without earning a single paisa in return - whether he or she is working in the military or in some social or charitable organization - is to be revered as a true icon of India. Those who profit from their activities, even if they are legitimate profits earned through hard sweat and toil - for instance through business management, sports or showbiz cannot be true icons - though they are far better than those who earn their riches through illegitimate means.

It is time that we all wake up to the utterly silly practice of exulting wretched people - those who have low morals, big egos, who have become alcoholics or chain smokers and despite their worldly status have not been able to cope with their personal problems. Such people can never be termed as great by any standard. Greatness has to come from within. It is a state of mind - not a state of one's bank balance. We need to give more public appreciation to those authentic heroes who truly deserve the deepest respect and admiration of the population. This will also encourage more people to imbibe nobler qualities and more mothers to remind their children that true greatness lies not in rupees or dollars or fame or talent but in self-sacrifice for a higher cause. Said the dauntless Bhagat Singh when he was condemned to hang from the gallows for revolting against British rule, "If I am hanged as a brave man with a smile on my face, Indian mothers will encourage their children to emulate my example...so that it will be no longer possible for the Satanic Powers of Imperialism to resist the Revolution." What a revolution will be brought about in India if each and every citizen remembered these intrepid warriors every day! What will India not achieve if only its one billion citizens would stop wasting their time on frivolities and flummery and got down to some serious work! Even if everyone can't do great things, at least everyone can do small things in a great way.

Come, let us today decide on our true heroes and begin to tread in their footsteps.

THE CASE AGAINST OBSCENE TV TELECASTS

All humans – in particular children and teens – are imitators at root. This is why advertising campaigns are so successful and also why 400 billion dollars are spent on advertising every year. If it didn't get people to do things they wouldn't otherwise have done, why would companies spend so much money on it? The sad thing is that people even imitate negative scenes which appear on their television and cinema screens – such as murder, violence, rape, suicide, defective mannerisms, smoking and drinking. Whenever somebody performs any of these negative actions, you can probably trace at least one of its nourishing roots to something he or she saw on television.

Said Emerson: "Sow a thought and you reap an action. Sow an action and you reap a habit. Sow a habit and you reap a character. Sow a character and you reap a destiny." Mature people realize that apparently small and innocent things can lead to grave consequences in the future. For instance, in Sweden, the sale of all war toys is prohibited. "Playing at war means learning to settle disputes by violent means," says a spokesperson. Since the censoring of gun scenes from TV and film screens in Jamaica, robberies dropped 25% and nonfatal shootings 37%! In yet another survey, nine out of ten prisoners admitted they had learned new ideas from TV and crime programmes!

Nevertheless, even if a person has the good sense not to get involved in copycat behaviour, the strains of peer pressure are sometimes overwhelming, particularly during adolescence and college life. If those people who undress in public are allowed in the least bit to become heroes and heroines, pressure by boys on girls (or vice versa) to do the same – or further – will surely raise its grotesque face at college, parties and elsewhere. Why have teenage pregnancies risen so steeply? And, in direct parallel, why have rape cases climbed so sharply, too? People call for the death sentence for such offenders but should we not also seek out what sources encouraged those people to commit those heinous crimes in the first place? Should not some sort of reform be introduced to clean up our media transmissions if it will help reducing unwanted pregnancies and averting horrendous crimes being repeated in the future? We need to restrain the trafficking of tainted thoughts and ideas – explicit or implicit – by means of the Internet, television, magazines and other media into the yet innocent minds of our youngsters.

Some people argue that no one should fuss about the *V Dare You* telecastings because people at the scene did not object. How dumb! Those people at the scene were numskulls! If they jumped into a well would you do so too? It's high time we began to use our brains a little more and started thinking more maturely about the long-term happiness of our children and future generations.

Lastly, if people and some television channels must dare one another, why not dare them to do something constructive and beneficial for our society? Dare a relative to give Rs.1,000 to a poor man! Dare a friend to go to a hospital and pray for the terminally ill. Dare yourself to help out at a school for the mentally handicapped for a day. Dare a television channel to telecast someone doing any of the above philanthropic dares. Dare the world to be prudent and sensible.

poor man! Dare a friend to go to a hospital and play for the terminally ill. Dare yourself to help out at a school for the mentally handicapped for a day. Dare a television channel to telecast someone doing any of the above philanthropic dares. Dare the world to be prudent and sensible.

THE WEST LOOKS EAST IN THE NEW MILLENNIUM

Cheers! Bravo! Hurrah! With merrymaking and much backslapping, we saluted the first rays of shimmering sunshine in the New Millennium. But wait a second. Were we gazing towards the correct horizon on that momentous morning? I mean, did we really superstitiously believe that the ball of swirling gases we call the Sun was going to solve all our woes? If so, it was not the dawn of a New Age of peace and prosperity at all, but an age of more starving children, poverty, endemics and epidemics, crime and misdemeanour. In a worst-case scenario we may witness the use of science and technology to liquidate billions of innocent people in a few murderous hours of psychopathic mutual destruction.

We can't afford to depend on enigmatic dates and epochs to cure our problems. We have to solve them ourselves. Can lasting peace, environmental protection or material riches really follow from international treaties drawn up on paper by the UN? In his book *War and Anti-War* Alvin Toffler notes that since the Second World War, we humans have warred more than one hundred and sixty times and more people have died in the carnage than the First and Second World War put together!

The basis of an authentic cure lies in addressing the issues of inner peace and riches such as self-esteem, contentedness, values and principles. This would have heralded the genuine commencement of a New Millennium – a New Era – one filled with world peace and material prosperity. But these subjects have been forgotten entirely!

It is evident we have put the cart before the horse: peace

ensues only from wisdom in the soul. This is the eternal message of the great seers and sages of Mother India. *Yatra vishwa ek needam* – "The whole earth is one nest" – and we are its siblings. This is why in its entire history of at least eleven millenniums or more, Mother India has never belligerently attempted military conquest over another nation!

The era in Europe belonging to the period between the sixth and twelfth centuries is generally known as the Dark Ages. In those days, the Sun looked as resplendent as it does today – if not more so. The flowers and foliage of the plants and trees were as varied and as enchanting as we experience today. Ecologically, it was a dazzling world of untold beauty and benedictions. Yet it was a dark, unlit world of appalling human destitution and suffering – a globe incarcerated in a veil of utter scientific ignorance, political and feudal clashes – all capped by the oppression and tyranny of a Church in aberrance.

Alas, similar horrors continue today, despite the fact we live in the age of the space shuttle and the home computer. Even the latest groundbreaking scientific evidence gathered from mapping the human genome, proving that all humans are nearly genetically identical, has done little to discourage people from warring with each other. It is not enough that light reaches us from the Sun. It needs to come from within.

What is required is a revolution of common sense, spiritual inspiration and a rapid reversal from selfishness and possessiveness to altruism and charity. There needs to be reform in the educational system, enlightening our children at a young age of the false messages, tricks and manipulative methods of television and advertisements. And there should be a massive uprooting of the hideous dictum: survival of the fittest. No individual or nation can survive or prosper on its own for long – *Om sahanau bhunaktu* – "Let us enjoy all things together." The bottom line is, either we live together or we die together.

Said British historian Dr. Arnold Toynbee, "It is already becoming clear that a chapter which had a Western beginning will have to have an Indian ending if it is not to end in the self-destruction of the human race."

So, let us look towards the eastern horizon - but not so far out as the Sun. We need look only beneath our feet at Mother India, who, as US historian Will Durant observed "is in many ways mother of us all." She is the cradle of human civilization. Let her continue to nourish her yet young child till it grows into the glorious and magnificent civilization it has the capacity to become.

CAN YOU GIVE LIFE TO ANIMALS?

VEGETARIANISM...

A visitor [illegible] and totally automated meatpacking factory in the US. Live and kicking cows were placed in at one end and came out packed in aluminium cans at the other. The visitor asked the proud manager, "Are you able to reverse the process, putting the cans in at the rear end and retrieving the live cattle at the front?" There was a blank expression on the manager's face. "If you cannot give life to the animals," continued the visitor sternly, "you have no right to take it from them either."

Members of the intelligentsia, however, perceptively pose the question: "Like animals, plants possess life, too. Why, then, do vegetarians kill them to eat?" This question arises from the widespread misconception that vegetarians blindly and indiscriminately opine complete non-violence towards all living beings. This is simply not true. If it were, the Ramayan and Mahabharat would not be Hinduism's most revered scriptures. The philosophy of vegetarianism is pragmatic and realistic. In

CAN YOU GIVE LIFE TO ANIMALS?

A visitor was being shown around a new and totally automated meatpacking factory in the US. Live and kicking cows were placed in at one end and came out packed in aluminium cans at the other. The visitor asked the proud manager, "Are you able to reverse the process, putting the cans in at the rear end and retrieving the live cattle at the front?" There was a blank expression on the manager's face. "If you cannot give life to the animals," continued the visitor sternly, "you have no right to take it from them either."

Members of the intelligentsia, however, perceptively pose the question: "Like animals, plants possess life, too. Why, then, do vegetarians kill them to eat?" This question arises from the widespread misconception that vegetarians blindly and indiscriminately opine complete non-violence towards all living beings. This is simply not true. If it were, the Ramayan and Mahabharat would not be Hinduism's most revered scriptures. The philosophy of vegetarianism is pragmatic and realistic. In

Hinduism, for example, one is permitted to consume plants for food – but only for the purpose of survival. Above that, purposeless killing of plants is as much a sin as the killing of animals. Similarly, if a tiger is charging towards you and you possess a gun, shooting the cat down would not constitute a sin because you did it for your survival. But if a person butchers a tiger or any other animal which is in no way threatening his or her life – like the poor one-year old Sakhi – which was recently slain and skinned by poachers at Nehru Zoological Park, Hyderabad, or like the elephants hacked to pieces for their tusks at Corbett National Park, Paterpani, one has committed a grave sin. Says the Bible, "Rule over the fish of the sea and the birds of the air and over every living creature that moves on the ground and for food, I give you every seed-bearing plant on the face of the whole earth." (Genesis 1:28-29) God has entrusted us to look after the animals of the world, not to slaughter them. For food, He has clearly given us only fruits, seeds and plants.

Ethical and spiritual issues apart, intelligent people can also discern the type of diet prescribed by nature for our bodies through a simple analysis of the body's physical makeup.

1. Human beings have teeth which consist mainly of molars and incisors that are adapted for biting fruits and chewing nuts and grains. Meat eaters such as cats and dogs have mostly sharp canines for gripping and tearing flesh from the body of their prey. Meat eaters also swallow their meals whole because they have little facility for chewing.
2. Human beings drink water in a similar way to cows and buffaloes – by putting their mouths to the surface of the water and sucking it in. Meat eaters such as cats and dogs drink water by lapping it up with their tongues.
3. Human beings have eight nimble fingers and two thumbs to pluck fruits, nuts and berries from plants and trees. Carnivores such as wolves, bears and tigers have short, razor-

sharp claws to kill and rip apart their prey.

4. Human beings, like comparable plant eaters, have intestines about twelve to fifteen feet long because much time is required to digest vegetables and there is little danger of them decaying during transition through the alimentary canal and poisoning the herbivore's body. In comparison, the intestines of carnivores are much shorter – usually about three to four feet – so that the rapidly decaying and potentially harmful flesh they have consumed can be quickly excreted. Furthermore, the stomachs of carnivores contain digestive acids twenty times stronger than that of human beings. This, again, is to dissolve the meat hastily before it poisons the carnivore's body.

One last argument pursued by incorrigible flesh eaters is that some avatars themselves went hunting or ate meat on occasions. My answer: "Are you an avatar? The avatars revived the dead, too, and therefore possessed the prerogative to take it back as well. We are not avatars, so we should follow the great saints of yore, all of whom were unwavering vegetarians.

DISEASE AND MEAT-EATING

Fill a scooter's fuel tank with rocket propellant and a rocket's fuel tank with diesel. What happens? The scooter turns into a fireball and the rocket stalls without lifting an inch off the ground.

Garbage in, garbage out. Tuck into an egg. What might you contract? Salmonella – a widespread form of food poisoning which is often fatal in young children and the elderly, says the *Journal of The American Medical Association*, 1988. Dine on fish and mussels. What might you ingest? Cancer-causing carcinogens from industries whose pollutants have pervaded much of the rivers and oceans of the world. Consume a chicken. What might you acquire? A deadly form of influenza called "Bird's Flu" which annihilated approximately 20 million people in Spain in 1918, 33,387 people in New York City in 1919 and thereafter, almost whole towns and villages in other parts of the world! A fresh outbreak in 1998 that was quickly contained claimed 6 lives in Hong Kong. Devour cattle, sheep or goat. What do you invite? Cancer of the digestive tract at best or at worst – a variant of bovine spongiform encephalopathy (BSE) or "Mad Cow Disease" – that ravages your brain. (Not to be confused with the recent outbreak of Foot and Mouth Disease in cattle abroad which is relatively harmless in humans). In humans, the variant of BSE is called Creutzfeldt-Jacob Disease or vCJD and is always fatal. It has claimed at least 94 lives in Britain and Europe already and will possibly claim millions more in Britain which has been feeding to its herds the processed remains of its own incinerated infected animals and exported millions of tons of the stuff to 80 countries including, Europe, Russia and much of Southeast Asia between 1988 and 1996. The world is standing on the brink of a potential pandemic – upon a ticking time bomb! Says French physician Dr. Frederic Saldmann, "We've been checkmated."

One of the first victims of vCJD was a bright, friendly and outgoing 20-year-old woman from Wales named Alison Williams in the mid 1980s. Gradually, her personality altered and she withdrew from people, including her family. Then, recalls her father, "A month before she died, she went blind and lost the use of her tongue. She spent her last five days in a coma." Three years ago in France, 17-year-old Arnaud Eboli – a martial arts enthusiast also contracted vCJD. His mother recalls how increasingly agitated he became, how he cried and how he used to sometimes scream at her saying, "I'm going crazy! I have mad-cow disease!" Later, he lost consciousness and today his emaciated body, still breathing, lies motionless in his bed at home.

However, unaware that BSE was being recycled in their

herds through feeding them infected nosh, people in Britain continued their traditional meat-eating lifestyles. The fatal disease was identified again only in 1996 after a number of deaths. Lamented *The Guardian* in its British editorial: "Beef is one of the great unifying symbols of our culture. The Roast Beef of Old England is a fetish, a household god, which has suddenly been revealed as a Trojan horse for our destruction."

But, we should realize that these terrible diseases are intricately connected to a society's eating habits and are almost unheard of in vegetarians. "Let food be thy medicine," advised Hippocrates. Even the AIDS virus which has already annihilated millions of lives and will certainly eliminate millions more, jumped from monkeys to humans only because people fed on monkey's meat or used their blood-extracts as aphrodisiacs. The sensible solution to these diseases, therefore, is to overcome the persistent thirst for the taste of flesh and to return to our natural vegetarian diet.

Ignore the blatantly false statements in meat commercials that meat and poultry products are good for you. Heed not the dubious statement that "unfertilized eggs are not non-vegetarian". And worry not about claims that meat and eggs contain essential proteins and Vitamin D. So do nuts and milk.

Let the fish, birds and animals live on. In doing so we will increase our own chances of survival too. Think wise. Think vegetarian. Think life.

herds, through rescuing them, infected most people in Britain continued their traditional meat-eating lifestyles. The fatal disease was identified again only in 1996 after a number of deaths. Lamented *The Guardian* in its British editorial: "Beef is one of the great unifying symbols of our culture. The Roast Beef of Old England is a fetish, a household god, which has suddenly been revealed as a Trojan horse for our destruction."

We should realize that the [illegible] diseases are intricately connected to a society's eating habits and are almost unheard of in vegetarians. "Let food be thy medicine," advised Hippocrates. Even the AIDS virus which has already annihilated millions of lives and will certainly annihilate millions more, [illegible] by monkeys to humans only because men fed on monkeys and used their blood extracts [illegible] these diseases [illegible] the persistent thirst for the taste of flesh [illegible] to our natural vegetarian diets.

Ignore the blatantly [illegible] statements in meat commercials that meat and poultry products are good for you. Heed not the [illegible] statement that "unfertilized eggs are not non-vegetarian". And worry not about claims that meat and eggs contain essential protein [illegible] vitamin D. So do nuts and milk.

Let the fish, birds and animals live on. In doing so, we will increase our own chances of survival too. Think wise. Think vegetarian. Think life.

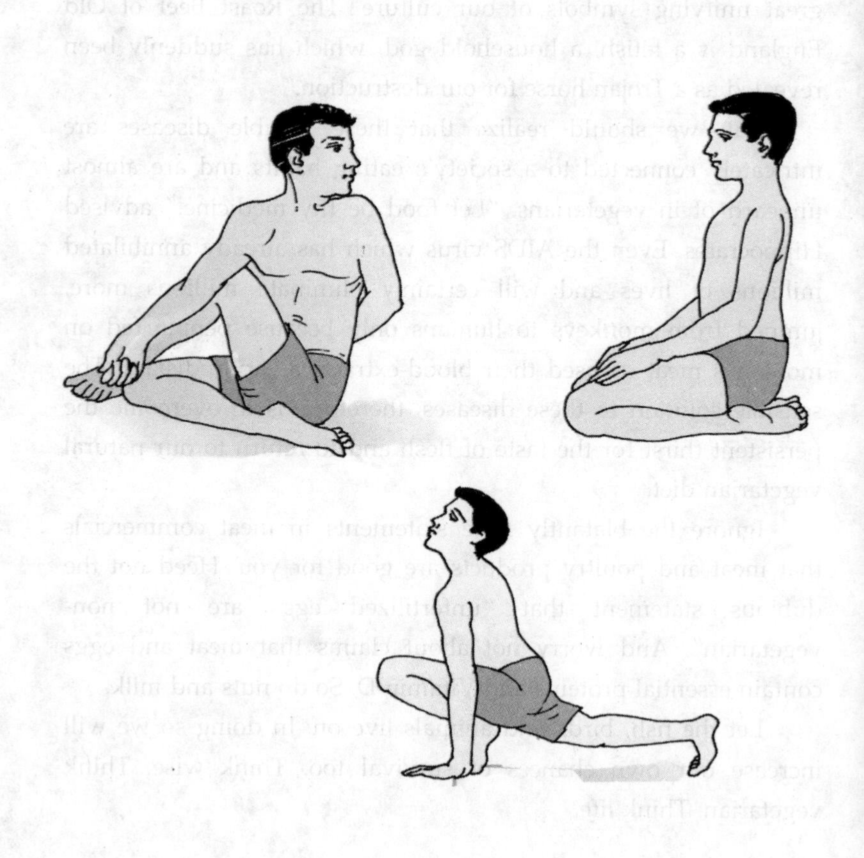

HEALTHY MIND, HEALTHY DIET, HEALTHY BODY

There was a time when the West used to ridicule India. They said India was primitive, superstitious and ignorant. But as US historian Will Durant later observed, India was actually the cradle of civilization and the country that gave birth to mankind's finest and foremost intellectual systems - algebra, chess, grammar, philosophy and the decimal system. Today, the West has begun to bow its head in gratitude before another of India's wonderful contributions to the world: Yoga exercises.

The word "yoga" comes from a Sanskrit root that means "to yoke" - which means to unify, to bring oneness. One of the primary functions of Yoga is to train a person to harmonize three things: posture, breathing and thinking. When this is achieved, a person attains peace with his (or her) inner self and with his surroundings. Nothing external or internal can disturb him and his body remains free from disease and his mind totally bereft of negative thoughts.

It is now well known that up to 80 percent of illnesses in the world have psychosomatic causes. In other words, an unhealthy mind leads to an unhealthy body.

In the 1970s, Dr. Herbert Benson of Harvard University conducted research which led to a medical breakthrough he termed "The Relaxation Response". The research concerned simple yoga techniques which regulate breathing and pulse to bring about a state of ease and relaxation. The results were stunning. 75 percent of insomniacs began to sleep normally again, 35 percent of infertile women became pregnant and 34 percent of sufferers of chronic pain needed to take fewer analgesics!

Similar medical breakthroughs have also been made by other doctors, such as Dr Bernie Siegel and Dr. Dean Ornish. Through a change of diet and mental attitude – with the help of meditation, visualization, and overcoming grief, grudges and grievances – literally thousands of patients have found their diseases (heart disease, cancer, AIDS, and other infectious diseases) to have been completely reversed or drastically reduced. In the US, the National Cancer Institute has found that patients who bounce back with a fighting spirit when diagnosed with cancer, have a vastly larger number of "killer T cells" – the cells which fight off cancer, than those who surrender to their illness with a resigned and submissive attitude. In London, researchers found that of the "fighters", 75 percent continued to live for another ten years! Of the non-fighters, only 22 percent continued to live that long.

Complementarily, Hippocrates – the father of modern medicine – used to say, "Let food be thy medicine." Latest research reveals that diet habits also contribute toward one's health and also to the condition of one's mind. Consumption of meat leads to colon cancer. It also leads to fatigue and lack of stamina – a fact supported by the great number of Olympic athletes who prefer a vegetarian diet. On the psychological side, eating meat desensitizes us to violence and killing: for nations that eat vast quantities of meat, violence and war become a legitimate means of achieving their goals. We need go no further than compare the non-violent, non-aggressive, gracious history of India with the belligerent and domineering histories of other nations.

The effects of smoking and drinking on one's physical health are also well known: heart disease, lung cancer and liver cancer are but a few. However, they also have a negative impact on our mental well being. Smoking and drinking can both contribute to depression, anxiety and low self-esteem. These, in turn, lead to more smoking and drinking! Alcohol consumption also reduces one's will power and self-control – most violent crimes such as wife or child abuse, rape and homicide are committed under the influence of alcohol.

The relationship between body and mind is like that of two close friends. They are inseparable. Whatever they do, they do together. If out of synch, the results are often disastrous, but when they cooperate with each other in perfect harmony, they work miracles!

THE HUMANITY OF VEGETARIANISM

Said George Bernard Shaw, "My stomach is not a graveyard for dead animals."

Disgust for the practice of slaughtering animals - particularly for food - is not new. Many great personalities of the past also chose to remain vegetarian - Plato, Aristotle, Pythagorus, Shakespeare, Leo Tolstoy, Leonardo de Vinci, Benjamin Franklin, Thomas Edison, Ralph Waldo Emerson, Charles Darwin, Albert Einstein and Mahatma Gandhi.

Today too, there exist a great number of famous personalities who have turned to vegetarianism: Paul Newman, Michael Jackson, Madonna, Sting, Carl Lewis, Whitney Houston, Elton John and Geoffrey Julianne - alias - "Ronald McDonald" - the famous clown of the McDonald's hamburger food chain. Julianne later resigned from advertising for McDonald's after realizing the inhumanity of the slaughterhouse, became a vegetarian and issued a statement to the press: "Meat is Murder."

People who eat meat should realize that animals are conscious too. The human mind is sickened and repulsed when it realizes this truth. Animals also have feelings just as we have. They love, care and worry as we do. They have a social hierarchy with a leader like we do. They have loyalties among the group like we do. They have affection between parents and siblings like we do. They can intuit death and fear it just as most of us do. Like us, they also have a life that they want to keep. Ex-Beatle and now pure vegetarian Paul McCartney was a meat eater until he saw the orphaned lambs of a sheep sent to the slaughterhouse. It was the last time he put meat into his mouth. "If animals could speak," said McCartney cradling one of the small lambs in his arms, "I think they would tell us not to eat them."

There are also many outdated medical theories circulating in society about meat eating – one of them being the claim that flesh is an essential ingredient of our diet if we are to remain healthy. But there could be nothing further from the truth! Today, after decades of research, doctors all over the world are recanting. Said Dr. William Castelli, Director of the Framingham Heart Study, "Vegetarians have the best diet. They have the lowest rates of coronary disease of any group... and have only 40% our cancer rate." There are other benefits of being vegetarian too. The risk of heart attack for a meat eater is 50% whereas for a vegetarian it is only 15%. Vegetarians also suffer less from arthritis, kidney disease, gallstones, asthma, heart disease, hypertension, strokes, diabetes and colon cancer.

There is another myth which has now been demolished, too: eating meat makes your body stronger than a vegetarian's. It doesn't. Al Beckles, Andreas Cahling, Bill Pearl and Covy Everson are all bodybuilders who have won the "World Champion", "Mr. Universe" and "Mr. Olympia" titles multiple times! In tennis, Martina Navratilova won "Wimbledon" nine times. Monika Montsho was "NW Woman Weight Lifter of the Year, 1991"! And all of these superbly fit sport's figures are pure and strict vegetarians!

What about the innocent, rich-in-protein egg? Surely there is nothing wrong with eating eggs? They're not quite so innocent, it turns out. It has been known since as long back as 1988 that eggs are a regular cause of serious food poisoning. In 1988 the *Journal of the American Medical Association* stated that eggs are a major cause of food poisoning throughout the world – even in countries like the US, Europe and UK. In America, for example, it was found that 77% of food poisoning cases had eggs at the root.

Lastly, some people argue that God created animals to be eaten. But the Bible and Hindu Scriptures at least – say no. Says the Bible, "Thou shall not kill." (Bible). "I give you every seed-bearing plant on the face of the Earth and every tree that has seed bearing fruit be your food (Genesis 1:29-31) "You shall not eat the fat of any ox or sheep or goat." (Leviticus 7:22-27) "Having well considered the origin of flesh and the cruelty of slaying beings, let one entirely abstain from eating flesh." (Manu Samhita) "Meat of animals is like the flesh of one's own son, and the foolish person who eats it must be considered the vilest of human beings." (Mahabharat. Anu. 114.11) "None shall eat the flesh of any animal even at times of famine or drought." (Bhagwan Swaminarayan; Shikshapatri verse. 15.)

Eating flesh is an ongoing atrocity committed by certain sectors of the human race – mostly for the purpose of satisfying their taste buds. But thankfully, times have begun to change and millions of people around the world are turning towards vegetarianism. Ultimately, said Leonardo de Vinci, "A time will come when men will look upon the murder of animals as they now look upon the murder of men."

Live and let live.

ENVIRONMENT...

There was a time when trees reigned the earth – every mountain, valley and plain – with swaying grace, towering trunks and canopying branches. These trees gave us oxygen to breathe, so that we could survive: without trees we would never have come into existence. And we still depend on trees today. They sustain water levels in the ground and through transpiration via their leaves transport water back into the atmosphere so that it can return in the form of rains. Trees give us fruits and shade. They give us protection from the environment and serve as a home and refuge to countless birds and insects. They even serve as a recreation ground for our siblings to play and learn.

But today, almost 90% of the world's rain forests have been annihilated. And every five years, due to deforestation we are causing 100,000 plant and animal life forms to become extinct. The havoc we have created environmentally in the last 40 years, say scientists, will take 10 million years to undo. One of the most worrying of environmental issues is "Global Warming". This is a type of global greenhouse effect affected by the increase in levels of carbon dioxide in the atmosphere from the burning of fossil fuels such as wood, coal and gas – and the cutting down of rain forests which absorb excess carbon dioxide from the atmosphere. It is occurring at such a pace that the polar ice caps have begun to melt, ocean levels are rising and in a worst case scenario, up 500 million people around the world may have to be relocated from the coastal regions of their countries within the next 100 years! And what about India or an island of simple landfill like Mumbai? We dread to even imagine the consequences for our children and grandchildren.

Man is inextricably bound to Nature. If he does not respect Nature, he does not respect himself. The biggest challenge therefore lies with ourselves. Above all, human survival the way we recognize it today will entail a renewed appreciation of Nature. Our ancestors viewed the whole of Nature – plants, trees, animals, birds, mountains, atmosphere, clouds and the Sun – as sacred and treated them with respect. Today we need a return of that reverence. As Harvard biologist Stephan Jay Gould puts it, "We cannot win this battle to save species and environment without forging an emotional bond between ourselves and Nature." Just as trees cannot abandon their roots, Man cannot abandon trees.

Man is inextricably bound to Nature. Recent research at

Pennsylvania found that patients in hospital wards whose windows faced an open sky or a tree healed faster than those whose windows faced a brick wall or another building! When man connects to Nature, he connects to himself. But when he mindlessly cuts a tree it is analogous to a woodcutter sawing the very branch he is sitting on. Man must begin to listen again to the voice of Nature which echoes his ancient past – to the rains as they patter upon the soft soil, to the wind as it whistles through the trees and to the birds and insects as they hum and warble amidst their breathing branches.

BAPS Swaminarayan Sanstha has already planted 1.2 million trees in Gujarat. But this will still not be enough to save our environment! Every citizen must actively participate in the project for it to be a success.

Every day of the year has to become "World Environment Day". So do yourself a favour and something for your future generations too. With every tree or flower you plant or nurture within your premises, office or home – you will be serving as a living lifeline bridging and supporting the ancient past and distant future.

Plant a tree. Water a flower. Get green. Stay connected.

OUR THIRSTING CHILDREN

Water is the life and soul of our planet. It is the life of life itself. Every single living creature on Earth and maybe, say scientists, even the entire universe depends on it. In fact, water is such a vital commodity that we are spending billions of dollars searching for it on Mars and the moon. Today wars are fought for land and oil. Tomorrow they will be fought for water. For those of us fortunate to get enough water to drink and bathe, its need in our everyday lives is usually not fully appreciated. But people staying in States such as Gujarat and in villages such as those in the Nandurbar district of Maharashtra today, know the value of water. Facing drought after drought and famine after famine, these people sometimes get barely a glass of water to drink each day. For them, water is like liquid gold; and its rains are like showers of diamonds which their children try to capture in their parched mouths.

People – elders and children alike – need water now! This cannot be overstated. Children are dying of thirst and malnutrition. We cannot keep waiting for the monsoons year after year. A more permanent and dependable source of water is imperative. The case expressed by environmental activists against the construction of large dams like the Narmada Dam may contain some atoms of truth, but those concerns are out of place in the context of the present crisis. Watershed and well recharging programmes are feasible theoretically, but in reality they are extremely inefficient because the logistics of educating and managing millions of villagers who will have to be involved in the programme is next to impossible. We have to remember that village farmers are not chartered accountants or civil engineers!

Some can't even read. Therefore we can't transform their village mindsets into metropolis mindsets overnight. Yet we still have a duty to feed them all – whatever has to be done or forfeited in the process.

Some activists protest that the dam will displace multitudes of tribal people. This is true. But, instead of blocking the construction of the vital dam, activists should focus their good efforts on ensuring that these tribal people are rehabilitated properly in an even better and more modern environment! Other activists protest that the dams will benefit the cities more than it will the villages. Even if this is so, the villages will still be obtaining a thousand times more water than the meagre supplies they're getting today.

Countries like the US may have stopped building dams now, but that, says *Time International* magazine (Earth Day Special Edition April-May, 2000), is mostly because there are no more rivers for them to build them on! Another reason is because they have already reaped all the benefits of their big dams, fed and educated their people and grown into a mighty economy because of it. If the US wanted to perform watershed and well recharging programmes now, it would be very simple indeed. The only other argument against large dams is the fall of the fishing industry. But the industry is an atrocity in itself! Stop fishing. Give water.

A man dying of thirst entered a restaurant at the edge of a desert. "I'm dying of thirst. Will you, please, give me a glass of water?" he asked the owner. "Wait 5 minutes," came the reply. "My man will give it to you." He waited. The water didn't arrive. He requested the owner several times, each time receiving the same reply – "Wait 5 minutes, my man will give it to you." After waiting more than an hour, the thirsting man crawled to the owner and asked, "Sir, for 5 minutes, will you be a man?"

WORLD PEACE...

WAR AND ANTI-WAR

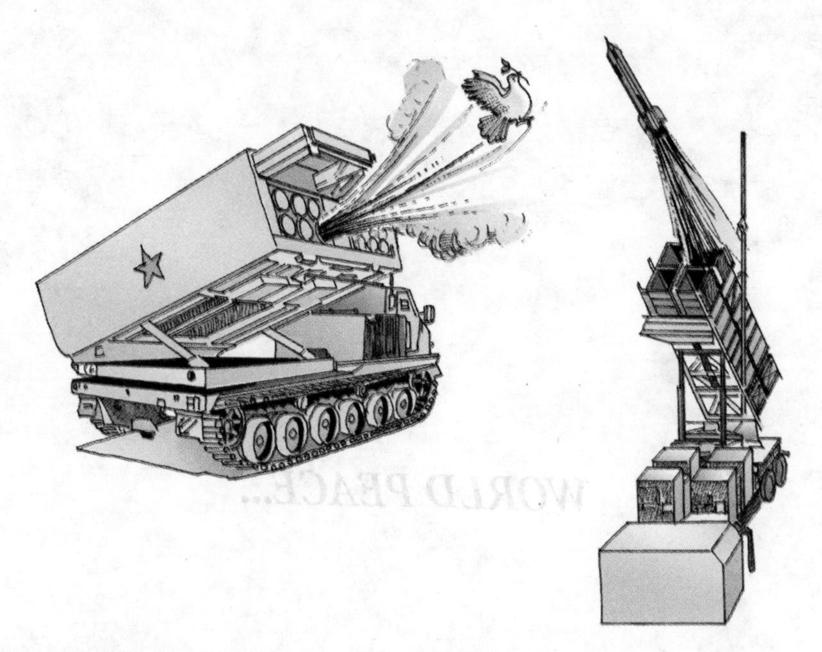

"The Earth looked so beautiful," said India's first astronaut Rakesh Sharma when he saw from his rocket our glittering blue planet suspended in dark, infinite space, "and I just couldn't believe that people were killing each other down there."

At any given time on this truly exquisite earth, some nation or group of people somewhere are at war with another. In fact, between the years 1945 and 1990, the world has known only 21 days of peace! And since then till today, maybe a week of war-free days may be added to that abysmal record.

After World War One, which killed 8.4 million human beings, world leaders congregated to form an alliance called "The League of Nations" so that no country would ever go to war against another again. Despite their inky, protracted commitments on paper, World War Two broke out between them just four years later in 1939! But the warring nations justified themselves asserting this was truly to be "the war to end all wars". After World War Two's culmination in 1945 and the gruesome deaths of another 55 million people worldwide, leaders of the world envisaged a dazzling 'New World Order' and the defunct League of Nations was replaced with the grandiose "United Nations Organization". World leaders then waxed eloquent that never would they or posterity have to witness the obscenities and atrocities of warfare again. Yet, between 1945 and 2000 the world has witnessed nearly 200 wars and the loss of an additional 41 million lives! Ironically, intellectuals after World War One claimed that another war between the great nations was impossible because of their economic links. But Germany and Britain shared sizeable economic interests with one another, yet this did not prevent the Second World War.

Most wars have very little to do with justice, economics or religion. Wars have usually been but a social symptom of pathological, neurotic minds; hearts filled with insatiable greed, ego, jealousy, prejudice, malice and fury; souls enveloped in utter darkness, disconnected from the holistic whole and blaming their feelings of misery on everything that appears foreign to them. The vicious backlash all this effectuates opens the gateway to hell on our otherwise heavenly Earth.

Truly, there is nothing more detestable and despicable than war and killing. Said US Vice-President Dick Cheney about Washington's decision to shoot down commercial planes heading towards US landmarks and not responding to instructions from the ground or Air Force, "People say that it is a horrendous decision to make. Well, it is." The fact is, war and killing in certain circumstances sometimes becomes inescapable - such as in India's own historical epics of the Ramayan and Mahabharat *dharmayudhs.* Such wars are a lesser evil than terrorism, tyranny and despotism. And they are a necessity to uproot them.

So let all India and every other justice-craving people in the world unite and arise in a single leap to wipe out this menace of terrorism and rid the earth of every terrorist's shadow. Let all freedom loving people stand by each other and brace themselves with warrior-like courage for whatever eventuality we may all soon have to confront. Let all mothers and fathers, children and friends determine not to shed a single tear during any period of this global crisis. A photograph was published during the Kargil crisis of a child sitting in the lap of his mother who was mourning the recent death of her beloved husband. He had been a brave pilot of the Indian Air Force and had been shot down by enemy guns. A tear had trickled down her cheek. Censured her son, "Mom, please don't cry. Daddy died for a good cause." Also maintain unalloyed and unswerving faith in God, for He is assuredly the Greatest. Justice will be done and will also be seen to be done! We must do whatever is possible and then leave the impossible to God.

Lastly, let us all examine our own personal lives and obliterate the similar greed, ego, jealousy, prejudice, malice and fury which fuels the feuds and fights within our own families and workplaces. Like charity, peace too should begin at home, should it not?

MATURITY: THE SOLUTION TO WORLD STRIFE

Not all the green and yellow meadows, sparkling streams and blooming, fragrant pastures of this Earth will end the folly and stupidity of mankind. Neither will all the mind-boggling supercomputers, glorious international space stations and prodigious feats of genetic engineering ever put an end to his irrationality. For under the guise of religion or patriotism, he will squander all his God-given natural resources and apply all his scientific expertise to obliterate his neighbour – even if it invites self-destruction or irremediable long-term harm to himself, his family or country.

Why this madness? Why the psychosis? Deep down in the hearts of many people, there exists a persisting malignant prejudice towards those who appear different from them. A geneticist will sermonize and wax eloquent on the genetic equality of all people, but he may twinge when he has to shake the hand of a person of another race! Humans develop prejudiced leanings towards almost every object they come into contact with – parents, relatives, siblings, friends, associates, magazines, newspapers, hairstyles, clothing, looks, careers and of course, race and religion. Indeed, even scientists are found not to be above such prejudices! Quantum Theory – the Crown Jewel of all physics – has five different and contradictory interpretations – each espoused by scientists of the highest credentials! This is because most of our scientific beliefs are subjective and founded in some form of bias.

Maturity is about growing above these biases. Maturity has nothing to do with the number of degrees or dollars one has amassed. Maturity is about seeing everything with an equal eye: with a deeply perceptive intellect and with steadfast emotions. Mind must not rule over heart and emotions must not rule over thought. Both must be balanced and the observing soul must remain the sovereign ruler above them. Neither heart nor thought should be discarded. They are a necessity, a requirement to guide our everyday lives and our actions in times of emergency. A person without a heart could not serve a dying person in an earthquake and a person without thought might end up hurting the very person he is trying to help. Forcefully extricating a person tightly buried beneath heavy debris, for instance, could snap nerve passages in his or her spine, causing permanent paralysis. In such a case, careful lifting of the fallen weight before rescuing the person beneath would be more prudent.

Peace and happiness comes only from such wisdom. Even in times preceding the scientific era and in parts of the world with low natural yields such as in certain areas of Africa, many people have known peace and happiness. In fact, even today, a remote tribe in Africa still exists which possesses no concept of war at all and has no word for war in its vocabulary! Applause to those people! They are some of the few true human beings remaining on Earth.

We have become doctors, engineers, businessmen, teachers, artistes, Pagans, Jews, Christians, Moslems, Buddhists, Jains, Hindus, Parsis, etc. but we have forgotten to remain human beings. In the burgeoning and multiplying roles we have to play every day of our lives, we have forgotten our basic identity, who we really are, what really counts. One of the consequences are the mounting tensions and strife around the world: family feuds, communal riots, terrorism, ethnic cleansing and bloody wars. We weep when natural calamities tear down our lives but we weep longer when it is fellow human beings who become the source of our sorrows: it is easier to overcome the anguish of losing a loved one in an earthquake or cyclone than losing a loved one in a bomb-explosion or riot.

We are the inheritors of a beautiful, blue planet. It is our home, and right now, our only home. Other life forms probably exist elsewhere in the universe. But the chances of man finding intelligent life elsewhere in our galaxy are low. Human life is even rarer than the Earth itself. Along with the air, soil and water of our planet, let us strive to preserve each other too.